BST

FRIENDS
OF ACPL

P9-CND-531

BECAUSE YOU CAN'T TAKE IT WITH YOU

How to Get Your Affairs in Order to Protect Yourself & Your Loved Ones

MARGUERITE SMOLEN

Foreword by Michael J. Brathwaite
CERTIFIED FINANCIAL PLANNER™

SELLERS
PUBLISHING

Published by Sellers Publishing, Inc.

Copyright © 2008 Sellers Publishing, Inc.
Text copyright © 2008 Marguerite Smolen
All rights reserved.

P.O. Box 818, Portland, Maine 04104
For ordering information: (800) 625-3386 toll-free
Visit our Web site: www.rsvp.com • E-mail: rsp@rsvp.com

President and Publisher: Ronnie Sellers
Publishing Director: Robin Haywood
Edited by: Mark Chimsky-Lustig
Production: Charlotte Smith

ISBN 13: 978-1-4162-0520-3
Library of Congress Control Number: 2008923778

No portion of this book may be reproduced, stored in a retrieval system, or transmitted in any
form or by any means, mechanical, electronic, photocopying, recording, or otherwise,
without the written permission of the publisher.

Author's note:
Please keep in mind that the contents of this book are for educational purposes only and should
not be construed as investment, financial, legal, or any other kind of advice or as an endorsement
of any information provided by people or organizations mentioned herein. Information and
opinions were obtained from sources believed by us to be reliable, but no representation or
guarantee, expressed or implied, is made by the author or publisher or by any person as to their
accuracy or completeness. The author is not an attorney, financial planner, or investment advisor
and this book is intended to provide only general, non-specific information. This book does not
cover all aspects or all issues related to the topics discussed. Any information contained in this
book is not intended to be used or relied upon to avoid taxes, penalties, or fees required by law
or to circumvent any law. Laws governing taxes, estates, wills, health care, contracts, banking,
investments, financial instruments, and other topics covered in this book vary and are subject to
change. Readers are advised to consult an attorney or other qualified professional who is familiar
with any applicable laws and the circumstances of their particular situation. Also, please note that
some names of individuals quoted herein have been changed to protect their privacy.

10 9 8 7 6 5 4 3 2 1

Printed in China.

Cover image credit: Don Hammond/Design Pics/Corbis

Contents

Foreword

CERTIFIED FINANCIAL PLANNER™ Michael J. Brathwaite
on what can happen if you don't put your affairs in order

As a CERTIFIED FINANCIAL PLANNER™, Mike Brathwaite, Vice President and Financial Advisor at Morgan Stanley and co-host of the Money Talk *radio show, has advised thousands of people on how to make the most of their finances before — and after — death.*

You truly can't take it with you! However, I've found that the idea of putting one's affairs in order is usually so fraught with emotion that people tend to put this necessary process on the back burner. That leads to vital decisions being made too late, if at all. Here are some of the common mistakes and unhappy scenarios that can result when people don't properly manage or dispose of their assets:

- **Neglecting to keep up with all of their assets.** Placing the burden of due diligence on heirs wreaks havoc with survivors.

- **Failing to update beneficiaries on insurance and other documents.** This can result in assets left to a parent who has already passed on — or even an ex-spouse.

- **Not designating who has power of attorney in the event something happens.** I had a couple as clients. They had been married for a couple of decades, but the husband kept most of his assets in his name. He was in a motorcycle accident and ended up in a coma. The wife couldn't pay bills because she didn't have access to money, and she didn't have power of attorney.

- **Designating a power of attorney is also important for single people.** Who will pay your bills if something happens to you? How will your family or friends access the money?

- **Appointing a health proxy — and keeping the health proxy language up to date.** Health proxies allow someone to speak for you if you become incapacitated or require terminal care. If you do not appoint someone as your proxy, siblings and other family members may disagree and fight over your treatment and care, wasting time and money. But even if you have a health proxy, be sure the language in it is current. HIPAA (The Health Insurance Portability and Accountability Act) regulates the disclosure of Protected Health Information (PHI). One (perhaps unforeseen) consequence of the HIPAA Privacy Rule, which went into effect beginning in 2003, was that an individual's private health information could not be shared without an individual's express, written permission, even with a spouse and/or close family members. The health proxy must not only specify the person who is to speak on your behalf, but it must also state that the medical facility can share information with that person that might otherwise be private.

- **Deciding to cancel insurance.** A classic example is an older person who says, "I have plenty of money; I don't need insurance." Upon death, the will goes to probate, and no one can get any of the money. The estate may be worth millions, but the assets are frozen, and there's no money available to bury the deceased. If the individual has insurance, the funeral home can obtain payment, but if there is no insurance, they'll demand payment up front. The survivors will have to pay funeral expenses out of their own pockets. With foresight, this can be avoided. For example, you could set aside some money for this purpose in an account held jointly by a survivor.

- **Assigning guardianship of children.** Even if you don't have a lot of assets, assigning guardianship of your children if something happens to you is very important — doubly so if you are a single parent. A lot of people struggle over assigning guardianship because they feel they have to choose between one person who is loving and caring and another who may be less emotionally available but who is better with money. In such cases, you might assign the more loving person the role of guardian and the more financially astute person the role of trustee.

- **Leaving money directly to a child who is in some way incapacitated.** A parent or even a good-hearted relative can make a serious mistake by making a disabled child the direct beneficiary of a will. Leaving money to a special needs child in a will may be well-intentioned, but this seemingly kind act often doesn't leave the child any better off. By doing so, you may deprive the child of Social Security, in effect reducing the benefits the child already receives. A better approach is to set up a special needs trust.

- **Having a will, but not properly titling assets.** Drawing up a will is half the battle, but equally important is properly titling assets. Titling assets — assigning assets to a trust or transferring ownership so that it is shared by the benefactor and a survivor — can ensure that assets automatically go to the survivor without going through probate.

- **Leaving the wrong assets to a charity.** An individual wanted to leave a million dollars to each of his alma maters. When he died, he left an estate that exceeded the amount exempt from inheritance taxes under the law. However, part of the estate was an IRA. If he had named the schools as beneficiaries of his IRA, as charities they would have been exempt from taxes. But he didn't — and now his children have to pay income tax.

- **Not having a will.** This will reduce the proceeds from your estate to any survivors and leave the disposition of your assets to the courts. Most people want to leave their assets to family, charity, and government, in that order. But when we do nothing, we put the government at the top of the list. People think that doing nothing is a passive act. Often, they don't realize that not taking action results in consequences that may run counter to their own best interests — or those of the people they love. By doing nothing, you've done something. You've written a post-dated check to the government and, by doing so, have guaranteed that the IRS will take half of your assets.

I recommend that you read *Because You Can't Take It With You* to make sure you're planning wisely for the future — and the well-being of your loved ones.

Introduction

Most of us don't enjoy thinking about taxes and death, even though we'll have to face them sooner or later. However, it's vitally important to have your essential estate documents prepared before it is too late. Getting your affairs in order is a liberating and empowering experience. When you have successfully organized your financial, health, home, and personal affairs, you are freer to spend more time with the people you love and more time doing the things that you love. You can live each day with confidence, knowing that if you become temporarily incapacitated, you will receive the best care possible. Your family will be able to pay bills, your assets will be protected, your associates can conduct business as usual, and you will return to health with your affairs in good order. At the end of your life, you will still have a voice in what takes place. In the months and years that follow, your wishes will still count, your assets will be managed and assigned as you have directed, and you will spare your loved ones needless pain and suffering.

But without estate planning, state and federal laws will determine how much of your hard-earned assets will be passed on, not you. The courts will determine who will inherit your money, your house, and your household goods, and who will take care of your minor or disabled children and your pets. The value of your estate will be subject to unnecessary fees and taxes, and what you had hoped to pass on will be greatly diminished.

If you are temporarily incapacitated, and have no plans in place, your family may be unable to pay for the medical care you need, and, though your health may improve, you could find yourself living a dramatically different lifestyle than you were accustomed to. You may return to a family torn apart by the stress of not being able to take care of someone they love or to adequately meet their own needs for a secure, stable home.

Despite the unfortunate consequences of not preparing for the frailties of old age and end-of-life, many people never get around to organizing their affairs. They may not fully understand that by not acting on behalf of themselves, their loved ones, and other beneficiaries, they have acted against their best interests. Frequently such procrastination is due to feeling overwhelmed by having to deal with vast amounts of paperwork and to make decisions about complex matters. Often, we lack the confidence to handle such weighty matters on our own and don't weighty matters on our own and don't know where to find help. But to live your later years with dignity and leave a legacy you'll be proud of, it is necessary to do some planning.

This book can help. It explains the important financial, health, and personal issues that must be addressed. In these pages, you'll learn how to organize your financial, health care, real estate, and personal records by breaking down these tasks into small, manageable steps that apply to your specific situation and goals. Practical guidance from expert professionals, informative definitions, tips and checklists, and insightful anecdotes from ordinary folks will help you to ask the right questions and give you the confidence you need to make decisions on your own — or to seek outside help when you need it.

Along the way, emotional and spiritual needs also will be addressed. You'll learn how to make end-of-life decisions that you can feel good about, ones that will reflect your values and goals and contribute to your legacy in a lasting way. And you'll learn how to communicate these values and goals, along with your final wishes, to loved ones, so they'll be able to implement your directives even when you are not able to guide them in person any longer. (If you are a concerned family member, this book also provides guidance for gently addressing difficult, end-of-life matters with an aging loved one.)

Whether you are planning for retirement or already retired, this book gives you the tools you need so you'll be able to face your later years with dignity and leave a legacy you can be proud of.

Get started now. Turn the page.

— M. S.

Chapter 1:
Getting Started

All right. You're determined to put your affairs in order. You know the benefits of preparing for the future, and you want to make life easy for your loved ones in case something happens to you. To that end, you're committed to gathering together the details of your financial, household, health, and other personal affairs in an organized fashion. But if you've picked up this book, you no doubt need some help getting the process started. Organizing your documents is the first step.

This chapter starts you on your way by answering the following important questions:

- *What documents should you have?*

- *How should they be stored?*

- *How will you communicate the location of your important papers to the people who should know about them?*

YOUR DOCUMENTS LIBRARY

One reason why people don't put their affairs in order is that gathering the necessary documents can be time-consuming. The longer we live, it seems the more paperwork we have. But like any task that is initially overwhelming, assembling your documents becomes much more manageable when you break the job up into small chunks.

If you affairs are quite complicated, you may wish to assign someone to help you manage this critical task — for example, an administrative assistant, if you own your own business; a lawyer, where complex legal documents are concerned; or a family member, if you simply want someone to share the burden. Planning the process is essential.

The 10 basic steps of document management are:

1. Identify the area that is or needs to be documented.

2. Identify the appropriate document.

3. Obtain the document (or a copy of it).

4. Get input from people (professionals or otherwise) about the document (for example, lawyers can help with wills, accountants with tax forms, human resources managers with employment benefits, insurance salesman with insurance policies, etc.).

5. Review the document and evaluate it:
   - *Should it be kept or tossed?*
   - *If kept, for how long?*

6. Decide where and how to store the document:
   - *What is the storage container?*
   - *How securely does the document need to be stored?*
   - *Should the back-up copy be stored in another location or be given to another individual for safekeeping?*

7. Record, or index, the document on a master log sheet. Documents may be kept in different places or require updates at different intervals of time, and a log sheet enables you to quickly identify the locations of various documents and the total number and kind of documents you have. Numbering your documents is especially important if you have more than one with the same name (for example, you may own more than one property and therefore have more than one deed). Be sure to also place a cover sheet on the document itself that identifies its number on the index.

8. Decide who should have access:
   - *Who should know where the document is stored?*
   - *Who should have access to the document? And, if so, under what circumstances?*

9. Notify appropriate persons about the location of the document, and provide them with the means to access the document (for example, keys or paperwork).

10. Schedule periodic reviews, updates, and maintenance.

WHAT DOCUMENTS SHOULD YOU HAVE?

The answer to this question is two-fold: first, you'll need to pick and choose what to keep from documents you already have on hand; secondly, you'll need to give some thought to your financial, family, health, and household needs and decide whether there are other documents that you need to prepare or obtain in order to ensure your affairs will run smoothly, both with and without you. The remaining chapters in this book will explore the rationale behind electing to have various kinds of documentation, so for now, we'll just set some general priorities.

The most important priority is, of course, to get started. For some of us, though, that's easier said than done. With so many of us finding ourselves swimming in papers, it's sometimes difficult to see the forest for the trees. If your time to devote to this project is limited (and whose isn't?), you'll need to choose what documents to focus on first. There are some documents everyone should have — a will, durable power of attorney, and one appointing a health care representative who can make decisions on your behalf if, for example, you become incapacitated. These should be your first priority, and, if you don't already have them, you should set a deadline for obtaining them in the very near future. That way, if something happens to you before you can get all of your affairs in order, you'll at least have the documents that have the most power to communicate and implement your wishes working on your behalf.

Other paperwork is important only if a particular situation exists, such as trust documents designed to assist a special needs child or other dependent. They are no less important than top-priority documents; however, like the parent in a plane who wisely puts on her own oxygen mask first before attending to her child, you should consider attending to your essential, first-priority documents before these needs-based, second-priority documents. Of course, depending on your circumstances, it may be prudent to ask your attorney to draw up these documents at the same time that the first-priority documents are being drafted. For example, an attorney may be able to help you draft a will and a trust document at the same time.

Finally, in third place come many documents that experts recommend that you keep for a variety of reasons — we'll explain why in more detail later in this book

— but that can take a backseat until priorities one and two are taken care of. For example, it is helpful to keep employment papers handy in case you need to look for another job, file for unemployment compensation, or verify benefits for current or end-of-life planning. But most experts would not assign this kind of paperwork the same high priority given to a will. Once you set up a working system to manage your documents, you can work on organizing these third-priority documents a little at a time over the next six months to a year.

The table on the next page provides a high-level view of this simple, but effective plan for categorizing your paperwork:

PRIORITIZING YOUR DOCUMENTS

Just like a hospital that does triage, you can prioritize your documents in order of which are most essential to attend to first. This system will help you to "chunk" this process, taking on the major paperwork in stages, so you don't feel overwhelmed.

PRIORITY	DOCUMENT	OBTAIN DOCUMENT WITHIN
Everyone should have/consider	• Personal identity papers • Will • Durable power of attorney • Health care or medical power of attorney • Living will	3 months from now
Needs-based	• Insurance policies • Real estate (deeds, mortgages, tax documents) • Trust instruments	3-4 months
Recommended	• Legal documents that pertain to transitions you've experienced (marriage and divorce decrees) • Contracts and settlements • Financial (bank, investment, and retirement account documents) • Employment information • School Records • Medical Records • Funeral Arrangements	6 months to a year

Where to Obtain Replacement Documents

As you start to organize your documents, you may discover that you misplaced some of them or can't find certified copies. Many important documents must be certified to be considered "official." For example, it's usually necessary to have a spouse's death certificate "certified" (that is, signed, and sometimes with an official seal) by a health officer or other official in order to file for survivor's benefits. A power of attorney (POA) is only effective if the person granting the authority is mentally competent; a physician may be asked to certify in writing that the grantor is mentally competent and fully understands the content of the document he or she is signing as well as how it will be used. The signature on the POA should also be notarized, so that the signature is less likely to be disputed. Identity papers, wills, deeds, and trust documents also typically require third-party notarization or certification. Obtaining copies of documents may be no more painful than calling an insurance agent and asking him or her to send out a copy of your policy. For other documents, however, the process is a bit more involved. On the next page is a chart of commonly needed important documents and where they can be obtained or replaced in case you lose any of them. When you speak to a clerk or go to a Web site to find out more information, be sure to ask or note whether a certified or notarized copy of the document in question is available or recommended.

Proving Your Identity

To obtain copies of official records you have lost or misplaced, proof of your identity will be required — ironically, even to obtain copies of certain proof of identity documents, you'll need one or more other documents to prove you are entitled to them. Depending on the document, you may be asked to provide one or more of the following:

- A valid photo ID, such as a driver's license

- State-issued non-driver photo-ID card

- Passport

- U.S. Military-issued photo ID

- Utility or telephone bills showing the applicant's name and address

- Letter from a government agency dated within the last six months

HOW TO OBTAIN/REPLACE CERTAIN DOCUMENTS

This chart below is a quick and easy look at where to obtain necessary documents for your personal file.

DOCUMENT	TO OBTAIN/REPLACE, CONTACT:
Adoption, birth, death, marriage, and divorce certificates	The local registrar of the municipality where the event took place, or the vital records section of the department of health for the state in which the event took place. Consult your state's department of vital records Web page for more information.
Citizenship/immigration documents	http://uscis.gov/graphics/formsfee/forms/. Also notify your country's embassy if documentation is lost. Military documents: U.S. National Archives & Records Administration at 1-866-272-6272 or 1-86-NARA-NARA; http://www.archives.gov/research_room/vetrecs/index.html.
Motor vehicle records	Your state's department of motor vehicles Web site for information; for an unofficial guide, check out www.dmv.org.
Passport	Your local U.S. Post Office; http://travel.state.gov/passport/
School documents	If it's for yourself or your child, call the school's registrar for fees (if any) and the appropriate contact information. Most likely, you'll need to request copies of these records in writing.
Social Security number/cards	Call 1-800-772-1213 to find the location of your local Social Security Administration office; http://www.ssa.gov/ssnumber/ for more information.

STORING YOUR DOCUMENTS

Once you've begun to collect all the documents you'll want to have, you'll need a place to store them. In some cases, you might need to store them in two locations. For example, you might want to keep original estate-planning documents, such as wills and trusts, with the attorney who drafted them, and send copies to any personal representatives you've appointed, such as the person who will be the trustee of your estate.

You can keep your own document copies, as well as most other records, in a safe deposit box or at home. The decision to keep copies at home depends on their importance as well as how easily you might want to access them.

Here is some information about safe deposit boxes and secure, at-home storage that can help you determine which documents you'd like to store where:

Safe Deposit Boxes

Safe deposit boxes are metal containers ranging in size between 3" x 5" and 10" x 15" that open with keys and are stored in the vault of a financial institution. They may be rented at a bank, credit union, or other savings institution for a modest annual sum of about $25 to $150, depending on size.

There are many benefits to having a safe deposit box. First, the box can't be opened without two keys present — the renter's and the bank's. Both keys are not the same, so if you lose yours, the box may have to be drilled open. (Therefore, be sure to keep the key to your box in a safe place, such as a home safe.) Renters must present an ID when they wish to access their boxes. In addition, banks typically keep signature cards on file, so they can verify the signature of the person accessing the box.

Documents that you might want to store in a safe deposit box include:

- Difficult-to-replace documents, such as birth certificates, deeds, contracts, stocks, bonds, and certificates of deposit

- Small valuable items, such as a coin collection or special pieces of jewelry

- Documents you may need in order to file insurance claims in case of fire or theft or damage by natural disaster, such as a real property inventory

- Items of sentimental value, such as cherished antique family historical documents, genealogical records, and photos or their original negatives

- Cash in the event of a disaster or emergency

Keep in mind that your box can only be accessed during the bank's business hours, so anything you might need suddenly at night or on a weekend or if you fall ill, such as a "living will" document, should not be kept exclusively in the box, but in a home safe as well.

Another reason to have secure, fireproof document storage in your house is that most safe deposit boxes are rather small. Even the largest don't hold the contents of a filing cabinet. A locked metal filing cabinet, especially one with some amount of fireproofing, is a good starting point for daily paperwork and current files needed for managing household and family affairs. However, you might want to create a more secure, fireproof area in another part of your house for long-term document storage.

Safe deposit boxes are generally more secure than a home safe or filing system. Because safe deposit boxes are located within a bank, they are protected by the same substantial security system that protects the bank's own assets. If you store collections or small valuables in a safe deposit box, ask your insurance company if it will reduce your premium for those items. But note that you do need insurance — items stored in a safe deposit box are not covered by FDIC insurance or the bank's insurance. The contents of safe deposit boxes are typically covered up to a certain dollar figure by a homeowner's policy, and you may also be able to purchase additional insurance if necessary.

Another benefit of a safe deposit box is privacy. Generally speaking, only you know what is inside your safe deposit box — unless, of course, you choose to share the rent with someone else. In order to have joint access to the box, however, a co-renter has to sign the rental agreement for the box as well. Just giving someone else the key won't guarantee access. After one is granted access to a box, he or she may view the contents in a private area designated for this purpose.

There are a couple of exceptions to these typical rules of access. When assets are legally frozen, as may occur in a dispute with the Internal Revenue Service (IRS) or other party, access to a safe deposit box may be put on hold until the matter is settled. If a law enforcement agency believes there is "reasonable cause" that you are hiding something illegal in your box, it may obtain a court order to open the box and seize the contents.

Also, access to safe deposit boxes is governed to some degree by state law. Be sure to find out what your state's policy is regarding access to your safe deposit box in the event of your death. Some states may allow an executor or co-renter access to the box for the purpose of obtaining the will and funeral and internment instructions. *However, because the bank's policy may be to seal the box upon the death of its renter, or the state may freeze assets, thereby requiring an official act such as a court order to open the box, it's generally recommended that you avoid storing original estate documents, such as your will or life insurance policy, in the box because there might be a delay in your burial and estate settlement.* In such cases, not even a power of attorney or a co-renter, who might ordinarily be granted unrestricted access to your box, would be allowed access.

It may be possible, however, while you are competent, to appoint an "agent" who could access your safe deposit box. The two of you would meet together with the bank representative, so that the bank could be assured you were authorizing the agent for this purpose. Again, check with your bank as well as an attorney or other knowledgeable person about laws in your state.

If you live in an area prone to natural disasters — for example, a coastal town in Florida that is routinely subject to hurricanes — it's a good idea to choose a bank that is some miles away from your home, so that there will be less chance it will be affected by the same weather emergencies.

For additional protection, you might want to seal items that could be affected by water damage in a waterproof container or sealed, plastic bag. Be sure to take photos of the box contents, record them on a list, and keep the inventory of the box contents and the photos in a separate location, such as a fireproof container or safe at home. In the rare event that a disaster of some sort happens, you'll have an easier time filing an insurance claim as well as contacting companies and governmental agencies for replacement documents.

Home Safes

A home safe offers convenience and easy access to your papers and other valuables, but to be sure you're not wasting your money, you'll need to ask yourself some important questions. First, why are you buying the safe? If it's just to protect these items from the eyes of prying family members, a locked metal filing cabinet may do. However, if you are concerned about protecting your documents and valuables in the event of a fire or to protect them from potential thieves, you'll need to shop carefully. There are many different kinds of safes out there. Though some sound impressive in their advertising copy, they may not be much better use to you than that locked filing cabinet. Start by considering:

Size: Think of your safe as a long-term investment. Make sure the safe you purchase will accommodate all of your needs — depending on what you are keeping in your safe, you may find you need a bit more room over time. If you are keeping large collectibles in the safe, you may wish to purchase a smaller safe for your papers and lock it inside the larger safe. The smaller the safe is, and the more portable it is, the easier it is for someone to take it. But it's also easier for you to grab if you need to leave your house suddenly.

Quality of materials and construction: Many experts recommend against anything less than 10-gauge steel. After all, if a petty thief can easily split the side of your safe open with a fire axe, it won't do you much good. Also look for a solid plate door, shielded lock box, and continuous welds, not "stitch welds," which may contain flammable filler. If a beam falls on your safe during a fire, the door may spring open or the seam split from the impact.

Lock: It's generally recommended to look for a lock that meets UL Group II or better certification. Some experts recommend rotary-combination dial locks as more durable than low-grade digital locks found on less expensive safes. Relockers can help — they are hardened pins that spring out if someone attempts to burgle the safe. It takes several hours of drilling to get past them. If you choose a manual lock, don't forget to spin the dial every time you close the door to ensure the safe locks.

Other experts feel that electronic locks offer more protection against an experienced safecracker. (Cheap keypads, on the other hand, may wear out, and if the lock fails while the safe is closed, you may have to hire someone to break into your safe.) If you are willing to spend money on a high-grade electronic or digital lock, they probably do afford the most protection. But remember to replace batteries once a year and reprogram your keypad frequently.

Whichever lock you choose, don't forget to record the access code so that you won't forget it. Be sure to give the code to the person you designate to manage your affairs (should something happen to you) as well, so he or she can get access to your safe's contents.

Location: It may seem obvious, but you shouldn't keep a small safe out in the open or in some other visible or easily accessed location, that makes it easy for a thief to find it and take it. Even a large safe located in a garage or one that's still attached to the pallet it came off the truck on, instead of being properly installed and bolted down, is relatively easy for someone to remove. Do place your safe in an area that's fairly hidden. The basement, if you have one, is not only out of sight, but offers added protection: in a fire, a safe located there won't be at risk of falling through a floor and possibly shattering from the impact of hitting the ground. If you install your safe in a corner, your foundation walls will offer additional protection on at least two sides. But make sure it's in an area where there are no combustible materials or power tools that will help a thief gain entry. Inside a closet behind a door with a dead bolt is another good place. That way it won't be visible to prying eyes. You can also install a security alarm as well as a smoke detector near the safe. The smoke detector may deter thieves because detectors may go off when they are trying to penetrate the safe with some kinds of tools.

Data and digital media safes: Since more and more of us are keeping electronic records on our home computer, this is a category worth mentioning. These safes protect their contents against electro-magnetic contamination and humidity as well as fire. In order to do so, they must maintain an internal temperature less than 52° C — electronic media, such as tapes and disks, can be destroyed at much lower temperatures than documents. A UL Class 150 safe offers protection for photographic film and Class 125 safes are designed to protect disks. Because of enhanced requirements, data safes tend to be expensive, however. An economical alternative is to buy a media drawer and store it in a fireproof safe or file cabinet.

Safe testing and certification: The independent product testing and safety certification organization, Underwriters Laboratories Inc. (UL), sets criteria for different kinds of safes. Look for a product that carries the UL mark or that has been independently tested to meet or exceed the UL specification that meets your goals (not just "to" UL criteria).

One last tip: A good safe can be expensive, so, if you don't have much money, scout the papers for businesses that are moving. You may find a used commercial safe for a very reasonable price.

Creating a Document Management System

Once you've decided on the kind of storage you'll use, you'll need to establish some kind of document management system to maintain its contents and to deal with the daily influx of paper. Your document management system should be designed to fit your lifestyle so that it requires minimal upkeep. Whether it's located in the kitchen, hall, or home office, the path from it to the mailbox should be straightforward and uncluttered, in order to avoid mail piling up in various places around the house. For security, you'll also need a document shredder. Since most communities these days recycle, a container dedicated just to this purpose is also useful. Finally, a calendar listing important dates related to documents (for example, the dates your real estate taxes are due, that school physicals will take place, that your insurance policy needs to be renewed, etc.).

Once you've established your document management center, it's important to develop a regular schedule for keeping your books and updating documents and records as you go along. In the end, this kind of routine will save time, money, and frustration. Again, a calendar with important dates can help you stick to a regular schedule.

You will also want to consider scanning your documents either for archiving or for bookkeeping purposes. It's important to do this regularly; if electronic updates are not made on an ongoing basis, so they can be traced chronologically, and if they don't contain exact reproductions of receipts, they may not be considered legitimate for tax verification purposes.

Online accounts present another issue that needs to be carefully addressed. Many banks and organizations now allow you to access or store documents online. Although online access and storage are convenient, it's recommended that you print paper copies of critical documents for storage in a safe deposit box, at home, or for your document emergency kit. Online payments and back statements should be regularly downloaded to ensure you have accurate and ongoing documentation of your accounts. Sometimes organizations only put information online for a few months. A Web site may go down temporarily, get hacked, or, as happened in the case of 9/11, get shut down due to a disaster.

Plan to copy this information on a CD, thumb drive, or other storage device at least quarterly. If you hook up an extra drive, you can image your computer and store a copy of its contents even more frequently. This copy of your computer's drive will be useful in case your computer crashes as well as for any emergency. Store media in a data or media safe. Store passwords, account numbers, and PINS so that you can access your information readily and so that your agent can access this information should you become incapacitated or die. This information should be written down and then stored in a fireproof safe.

The Annual Review

Once a year, plan to review items in the current file and temporary files to determine whether they should continue to be stored or whether you can shred and discard them. Some papers are extremely important and must be kept permanently. Others will be kept only temporarily. As you go through your files, consider whether existing documents are needed to deal with an ongoing situation, whether they can temporarily go into storage for some period of time, for example, three to seven years (the length of time it's recommended you keep various tax records), or whether they must be kept permanently. Any critical documents that would be needed in the event of an emergency should be reviewed at least once a quarter. Also review and update your information whenever a major life event occurs (for example, marriage, divorce, becoming a parent, moving, retirement, changing jobs).

Documents and the IRS

While most documentation should be reviewed annually and updated, with the out-of-date documents tossed when they are no longer useful (unless there is a sentimental reason to keep them), bear in mind that the IRS has up to three years after you file a return to audit that return; keep your personal and business records at least that long. Maintain them for four years if you do income averaging, to prove taxable income for four base years. Also keep them four years if your small business or farm has employees. In addition, the IRS has up to six years after filing to audit returns where 25 percent or more income has not been reported. If the IRS suspects someone of fraudulently filing returns, the audit period is indefinite. (For more information, see IRS Publication #552, "Record-keeping for Individuals.") You may also need real estate agreements, receipts, and cancelled checks to claim capital gains exclusion when selling a house for more than the amount it cost you. We'll review how long to keep specific documents in the following chapters.

COMMUNICATING THE LOCATION OF YOUR DOCUMENTS

The simplest way to inform people of the location of your important documents is to prepare a document inventory list. Because different kinds of documents require different kinds of storage, a document inventory list that includes who has access to the document or is storing your documents for you can be helpful when it comes to accessing specific documents at any given point in time. Circulate copies to your attorney and family members, so they can easily access this information if something happens to you. The charts at the opening of each of the following chapters will help you compile this "My Documents At-A-Glance" inventory.

Where to Go from Here . . .

As you start to think about the documents you have and those that need to be obtained, you will probably start to realize that you have to take some steps to address your family's future needs and will want to draft other documents to ensure the continued well-being of your family and your estate. For example, many people spend significant chunks of time filing and storing old utility bills, but neglect to keep track of important medical papers that could save their life in an emergency. Parents of children will save coupons to buy their child the newest popular toy, but never get around to meeting with a life insurance provider to make sure they are adequately covered and that their child will be provided for in case of an emergency. As you work your way through the chapters in this book, you'll learn why a will is critical, even if you think your estate is "tiny," why you might want to set forth your wishes in a "letter of intent," the importance of specifying your end-of-life-care decisions, and more. By paying attention to these details now, you will prevent endless difficulties and stress for your family in the future.

RESOURCES

(Note: All resource information in all chapters is current as of the printing of this book.)

ORGANIZING SUPPLIES

Archival Methods Archival Storage Products
(Archival storage products)
Web site: www.archivalmethods.com

The Container Store®
(Storage containers and organizers)
Web site: www.containerstore.com

FactoryEXPRESS®
(Supplier of home safes and document containers)
Web site: www.factory-express.com

UniKeep™
(Binders and organizers)
Web site: www.unikeep.com

KITS

CorpKit Legal Supplies
46 Taft Ave., Islip NY 11751
Phone: 888-888-9120; Fax: 888-777-4617
(Offers the HomeOwner's Record Keeping System
and various forms and kits)
Web site: www.corpkit.com

Day Runner®
(Estate record planners, various document
organizers and storage containers)
Web site: www.dayrunner.com

Knock Knock
(Medical, home, personal library and other organizing kits)
Web site: www.knockknock.biz/commerce/kits.html

NOTES

Chapter 2:
Financial and Estate-Planning Documents

MY DOCUMENTS AT-A-GLANCE

Fill in the chart below to keep track of where your critical documents will be stored and who will have access to them.

DOCUMENT	LOCATION	ACCESS/COPY GIVEN TO
Will		
Power of attorney		
Living will		

YOUR IMPORTANT DOCUMENTS

Most experts consider the three kinds of documents above the foundation of any basic estate plan.

Through a *will* you can name beneficiaries and transfer assets to them, structure the distribution of your assets, and appoint someone to oversee that distribution (an executor). A will typically includes:

- Your name

- Your address

- A summary of your assets

- A summary of debts and a direction to cancel them, and a direction to cancel any debts someone may owe you, if you wish

- Names of any beneficiaries, for example, family members, friends, and charitable organizations, and any alternate beneficiaries, in case anyone predeceases you

- Description of any specific bequests ("I want cousin Jane to get mom's silverware")

- Language about trusts, if you've decided to establish any trusts

- The name of the person you want to manage your estate (the executor)

- The name of any guardian you want to appoint for minor children, and an alternate, if the first designated guardian becomes incapable of performing his or her duties (or is unwilling to)

- Your signature

- The signature of witnesses who are competent, of age, and not beneficiaries (it's a good idea to also have a notary witness the signatures)

If you're single, you'll need to specify your beneficiaries in a will, otherwise time and money will be wasted having the state determine that your closest relative should get your assets (and who that is). Depending on the laws of the state, if you're married with minor children and die without a will, state law may give the bulk of the estate to the children, instead of the parent who will be responsible for caring for them — opening up the possibility that the children may fritter away the assets. For those with children, the will is also the place to name a guardian in case of an untimely parental death; otherwise, your children could end up being raised by someone you wouldn't have chosen. The will and its contents, including any appointments of guardians and executors, must be probated — presented to the court, validated by the court, and processed in accordance with the law at your death.

The *power of attorney (POA),* the next most important type of document on the list, appoints someone to act on your behalf. A *general power of attorney* can be used for things like handling financial matters (banking transactions, buying or selling property, purchasing insurance, entering into claims, filing your tax returns). The person you choose to authorize to act on your behalf is up to you, and you can decide to limit his or her authority to certain areas — such as finance, real estate, or health care. (For example, a *health care power of attorney* or *health care proxy* appoints someone to act on your behalf in health care matters.) You also can decide to authorize someone to act on your behalf for a limited time period, such as sixty days from date signed.

If you want to make sure a POA will remain in effect if you become incapacitated or incompetent, you can draft a *durable power of attorney.* For example, through a durable power of attorney you can appoint someone to handle your finances should you become mentally incompetent. You can appoint someone else to make health care decisions on your behalf if you become incompetent through a *durable power of attorney for health care.* Items typically included in this document are provisions for the removal of a physician, the right to obtain medical records, and the right to have the patient moved to another treatment facility, obtain other treatment, or to be discharged against medical advice.

You can specify that these POAs would only go into effect if two or more doctors certify that you are mentally incapacitated. In some cases, individuals may sign a POA for convenience's sake — to appoint someone to manage their finances on a daily basis if they are out of the country, for example. In such cases, a durability provision may be included to allow for the POA to remain in effect if the person signing it is later deemed incapacitated. These documents must be drafted and signed while you are deemed competent (you might get a letter from a physician attesting to this fact at the time of signing). Because your appointed agent may not be able to serve as your POA when the document goes into effect (suppose they, too, become incapacitated), you should also appoint a successor agent. You can revoke a power of attorney document; the legal term for this is *revocation of power of attorney.*

Another type of advance directive (or document expressing your wishes in advance of an event that is yet to happen) is the *living will.* The living will is used to explain your preferred treatment and end-of-life care, such as any life-sustaining or extending treatments, to your physicians, care providers, and health care POA. Both the health care POA and the living will are sometimes combined into a single document called an *advance health care directive.*

If you do no other estate planning, experts recommend that you obtain these documents for yourself. Sample forms are available online or in any office supply store for minimal cost. You also can use these forms to draft documents, together with supporting records, such as those listing your assets, and then take them to an attorney for review. The more work you've done upfront, the less work the attorney may have to do, which should reduce your costs. Many attorneys charge a reasonable flat fee to draft a simple will, and, even if that's all you need, you would do well to consult one because state and local laws vary, and an attorney familiar with both can advise you properly. Even if a particular generic will form is legal in your state, it may not be the best way to structure your asset distribution, which depends on your particular situation and not those of an average "generic" person.

To facilitate estate administration, you may wish to draft a *letter of intent.* This isn't a legal document, but a personal guide that lays out where the documents, which are needed to conclude your affairs, are located — the will, financial, real property inventory documents, and so forth — so your loved ones won't have to hunt them down. It can include a list of the professionals, legal and otherwise, that you have relied on and that your loved ones may wish to contact for information or for advice. This letter can also provide additional information about your preferences regarding how things should be managed at your death, including care of minor children, pets, and other dependents, and information about preplanned and paid-for funeral arrangements. You should include your letter of intent with your most important documents so they're gathered together in one place and easily available.

"I feel much more comfortable now that I've met with an attorney and filled out paperwork that gives instructions for how to handle my care should I become incapacitated. I was horrified watching family members fight over Terri Schaivo on national TV. I was especially worried that someone with religious beliefs different from my own might want to prolong my life unnecessarily. By filling out the forms provided by my attorney, I am at peace, no matter what — or when — something happens."

— *Stella, age 69*

FINANCIAL AND ESTATE PLANNING

This comprehensive chart will help you coordinate how long you should retain your statements and records, and where you should consider keeping them.

DOCUMENT	LOCATION	KEEP FOR
Bank account statements and other records	Home file; keep copies of any ATM or debit cards carried in your wallet there, too	7 years for tax purposes
Beneficiary documents	Fireproof container at home or home file	While in effect
Checks (cancelled)	Home file	Minimum of 3 years if it's a non-tax-deductible purchase or the warranty does not last longer
Credit card records, including agreements, statements, and payment records	Unused cards and list of cards, companies, and contact information, in safe deposit box or fireproof container at home	Duration of account or 7 years for tax purposes
Durable power of attorney (financial)	Needed by your agent as soon as he/she starts making decisions; if that time has not yet arrived, keep the original on file with your attorney or in a fireproof container at home.	Until it is revoked by the Principal, or until the Principal's death
Employment records	Home file	Permanently
Financial document inventory	Safe deposit box with a copy in home file	Until updated
Insurance policies (life, annuities) and records	Keep a list of policies in your safe deposit box; policies in your home file	Minimum of 4 years after the policy expires

DOCUMENT	LOCATION	KEEP FOR
Investment (stocks, bonds and other securities) and savings certificates	Safe deposit box; copies in your home file	Three years past sale or longer if needed for tax purposes (usually 7 years)
Investment records, including buy and sell orders, cancelled checks, and statements	Safe deposit box; listing in the home file	3 years past sale
Loan agreements	Safe deposit box or fireproof container at home	Until the obligation is satisfied or longer for tax purposes (usually 7 years)
Pension documents	Safe deposit box or fireproof container at home	While in effect
Retirement account records (IRAs, 401Ks, etc.)	Safe deposit box or fireproof container at home	Permanently
Tax returns, including supporting receipts and documentation of income, deductible expenses, and tax forms and payments	Safe deposit box or fireproof container at home	Minimum 7 years after filing
Trust papers	Signed original with lawyer. Keep copies in a safe deposit box or fireproof container at home. Provide copies to trustee.	While in effect
Will	Signed original with lawyer. May be filed with probate division of circuit court in some states. Keep copies in a safe deposit box or fireproof container at home. Provide copies to executor.	While in effect

CHECKLIST FOR WRITING A WILL

❑ To be legal, the individual writing the will must be of "sound mind and body." If your competence may be questioned, you can have a physician make an examination of your ability to reason and to understand the nature of the document you are signing and the issues it addresses, including the proposed distribution of specific assets to the heirs specified, and then confirm in writing that you are competent.

❑ Start by collecting all of the information regarding your assets — bank account statement, investment paperwork, real estate deeds, asset inventories, insurance policies, etc. Also collect all of the information regarding your liabilities — debts, loans, and any financial judgments that may have been entered against you.

❑ Name your beneficiaries and assign them assets, appoint guardians for minor children, nominate a personal representative for the estate (executor), and generally describe how you want your estate to be settled. You can use an online will form or software program to do this or have an attorney draft the will for you. It's important to follow a standard format in your will and to type it; most states will not accept a handwritten (holographic) will.

❑ Have the will signed by two or more witnesses over the age of forty who are mentally competent, are not beneficiaries or related to you, and who would be willing to confirm they witnessed the signing in a court of law if necessary. Check your state's law to be sure you do not need an attorney to authorize your will; a few states require a will to be notarized by an attorney; most do not.

❑ It's recommended that you have the will reviewed by a lawyer if you did not hire one to write it.

❑ File the will with your lawyer and put copies in secure storage as well.

❑ Review periodically and make alterations (called a *codicil*) as necessary.

ADDITIONAL ESTATE-PLANNING GOALS

Estate planning isn't limited to obtaining a will, a power of attorney or a living will, however critical they may be. While assigning people to manage your affairs if you're ill and transferring your assets to designated beneficiaries upon your death are important steps, a *comprehensive* estate plan accomplishes much more. Ideally, an estate plan can help you grow your assets and to protect them in the years to come, so they'll be available for you when you need them or to pass down to your beneficiaries. Ideally, working with a financial planner, accountant, and an attorney, you can create an estate plan to help with the following:

Funding:

Estate planning helps you save and invest, so that you will be able to take care of your needs through end-of-life and have an estate to pass to loved ones or causes you wish to support. An estate planner can suggest funding vehicles (for example, insurance products and investments) to help you invest a portion of your income to fund your plan.

Risk management and capital preservation:

Through various estate-planning and financial tools, you will have an assured source of income should you face disability or serious illness. Working with a financial planner can help protect your financial status against inflation and economic downturn.

Protection of your assets against creditors and other liabilities:

Various protection vehicles help reduce your exposure in the event of an accident, tax, or creditor claim. These include such asset-protection techniques as transferring assets to a spouse and establishing trusts for children or other family members, homestead exemptions, life insurance, assets held in joint tenancy, and limited partnerships. Because some of these options have a limited application and may require you to give up certain rights, you'll need to consult with a professional to understand the advantages and disadvantages of these various options, when to apply them, and which of them, if any, are useful in your particular situation.

Maintaining liquidity:

Estate-planning vehicles, such as insurance, provide immediate financial liquidity. They enable the prompt payment of your debts so your survivors don't have to depend on their own financial resources to handle your burial and other estate administration expenses prior to estate settlement. Typically, the state Department of Health regulates burial, and if someone dies without making his or her own arrangements, the state requires the surviving spouse to arrange for burial and pay for it. If there is no spouse, the state will determine who the next of kin is and who is responsible for payment, or arrange for burial with the deceased's assets. If someone is truly without relations and assets, and no one steps forth to accept this responsibility, the state itself may pay for disposal of the remains.

Reducing your tax liability:

Many types of taxes can affect the distribution of your estate as well as the finances of your beneficiaries; for example, federal and state gift and income taxes, federal estate taxes, and state death taxes. Generally speaking, the state death tax is a tax based upon a person's right to receive assets, such as property or money, that the decedent owns at the time of death. The federal estate tax is a tax upon the total value of the property owned by the decedent. Inheritance tax returns must include a list of the assets and liabilities. The federal estate tax has gotten a lot of press recently, due to the 2001 Tax Act, which is supposed to eliminate estate taxes by 2010. It's unclear what will happen after 2010; however, at the time of publication, these taxes would only be in remission for a year, after which the taxation would return to pre-2001 levels. This tax act and subsequent changes to the law may have an impact on state death taxes as well. State death taxes vary, but often include taxes on the estate that are typically equal to a state death tax credit allowed under the federal estate tax law (also called a "pick-up" tax) and an inheritance tax that may vary depending on how close a relation the beneficiary was to the deceased, with the closest relations having the greatest exemption from the tax and the smallest rate. You must contact a tax attorney to find out the current state of affairs. Your advisor also can discuss ways to specify how and when your beneficiaries will receive your assets and recommend some other estate-planning tools that can help achieve a transfer of assets so that less of them are taxed. If an estate is properly structured, it may pass tax-free to beneficiaries. For example, if the spouse is willing, he or she may inherit assets from a wife or husband without paying taxes, then sign over assets to the children, so they won't have to wait to inherit them from the second parent and, in effect, pay a second inheritance tax on this money.

Reducing probate costs:

Probate is a fancy term for the court-supervised process by which a court determines that a will is the deceased's final direction for the distribution of his or her assets. It includes appointing a personal representative of the estate, the gathering of any assets, payment of debts, taxes, and administration costs, and, finally, the distribution of those assets to assigned beneficiaries. Planning can reduce the cost of taxing the state and probating the estate, since these fees are often calculated based on the estate's size, and your advisor may be able to suggest ways you can reduce the size of the estate (that is, limit the assets that pass to beneficiaries through the will and are therefore subject to inheritance tax). This is typically achieved through the use of life insurance products, trusts, contracts or deed assignment, or effective application of laws involving jointly owned property, rights of survivorship, lifetime gifts, and pension and retirement plan beneficiaries.
As these goals suggest, the main purpose of estate planning is to protect assets on behalf of your heirs. If you choose to leave money to your survivors, you'll want to make sure you're doing the kind of smart financial planning that will preserve as much of the value of your assets as possible. This can be achieved by facilitating estate administration and settlement through careful organization of documents and the preparation of detailed financial and personal property inventories.

WORKING WITH ESTATE PROFESSIONALS

Of course, when it comes to prioritizing estate-planning goals and actually drafting estate documents, such as wills and POAs, you'll need to consider the specifics of your own situation. Your relationships, your financial status, whether you own property, and how old you are, as well as your lifestyle, beliefs, and goals, all can affect how you might want to structure your estate plan and what you want to address in your estate-planning documents. That's where the challenge comes in and why you might want to consult a professional advisor to help you sort through your options instead of just downloading a form from the Internet or using a pre-printed, generic form or software program from an office supply store.

After learning the details of your particular situation, your legal and financial advisors may recommend that you augment the basic estate-planning documents discussed above with other tools, such as trusts, insurance products, certain kinds of banking accounts, and more, to help stretch your estate dollars further and to ensure your assets are managed in keeping with your wishes after you die. For example, they may suggest you take advantage of the following tools:

• Marital deductions - married couples who are U.S. citizens benefit from the federal gift and tax law, which allows a tax-free transfer of an estate to the surviving spouse as well as the "equalization" of individual estates to obtain the total exclusion benefit. There are also trusts that help pass assets directly to spouses outside of the will.

• Insurance - life insurance in itself can be used to create an estate, as well as pay any debts you've left, while liability insurance can help protect your assets.

• Certain financial instruments - retirement and some investment accounts and life insurance products, which require you to name beneficiaries, allow for benefits to be passed directly to the beneficiaries named on the instruments rather than having to designate them as such in the will.

• Property ownership as a joint tenant or tenants by the entirety, which allows the property to automatically pass to the other person upon death without needing to be transferred in a will as part of your estate.

• Trust accounts, which can help protect your assets from "spendthrift" beneficiaries, or hold them for distribution at a later date or on an as-needed basis, so as to reduce tax liability or preserve the recipient's other benefits (as in the case of a disabled child receiving Social Security benefits or an aging parent receiving Medicaid).

• Self-employed business owners may protect their personal assets from business creditors (and vice versa) through incorporation, or establishing a limited partnership, or limited liability company (LLC) to protect personal assets.

• Payable-on-death accounts, which transfer their contents to the person named by you, upon your death.

Another reason to consult with an advisor is to help you provide appropriate direction about your finances or health care to the people you appoint to work on your behalf (such as a power of attorney or health care proxy). While you may authorize them to make decisions, and you've chosen them because you trust their judgment, you'll want to provide them with guidance. A knowledgeable estate professional, such as an attorney, can help ensure your documents are phrased correctly and are in the right hands when these decisions are made, and can also recommend steps to take to ensure that the content of these documents is respected. Since laws differ according to state, and sometimes even municipality, be sure your attorney is familiar with your local laws and institutions — as well as other state laws that may affect your estate plan. One way to do this, in addition to simply asking about the length of time she or he has practiced locally, is by reviewing your attorney's resume for education, participation in organizations, and legal publications in the field of specialty.

CHOOSING AN ESTATE-PLANNING PROFESSIONAL

Professional advisors may specialize in different aspects of estate planning and hold different degrees or certifications. Estate-planning professionals are also compensated in a variety of ways. For example, a fee-based advisor may charge either an hourly rate or a percentage of the assets managed or the income produced. Some may work for a company and earn an annual salary, in which case you may pay the company that pays their salary a service fee. Or they may receive a commission based on the products and services you buy. Some people feel it's best to pay a rate for "unbiased" advice from someone who won't earn anything off the products you buy, others feel that if an advisor earns a percentage of the income from an investment, he or she will have more of an incentive to help you make money on the investment. Still other people feel certain they wish to purchase certain products or services and would rather have the compensation incorporated into the fee for the product or service. Only you can determine the kind and number of professional advisors as well as the compensation plan that's best for you.

There are a variety of professional advisors available to help you with different aspects of your estate-planning needs. Here are some of the different specialties you can choose from and the qualifications you should look for:

Accountants provide information about tax laws, your specific finances and tax returns, and options for tax-advantaged management of your financial affairs. Certified Public Accountant (CPA) Boards of Accountancy are listed with the National Association of State Boards of Accountancy and the American Institute of Certified Public Accountants.

Attorneys or lawyers provide advice on legal matters related to estates, including information about tax laws, medical directives, powers of attorney, and health care proxies. They draft legal documents, such as wills or trusts. Attorneys also help with legal aspects of estate administration after the benefactor dies. They draft and file documents to probate the will; advise the estate administrator about legal and tax matters; represent the executor in probate court; and prepare and file tax returns on the estate's behalf. They have a law degree and a state license. If you are primarily concerned with estate planning, you may also look for someone who specializes in wills and trusts, such as an Estate Planning Law Specialist (EPLS) with certification from the National Association of Estate Planners & Councils Estate Law Specialist Board, Inc. A Certified Elder Law Attorney (CELA) certification from the National Elder Law Foundation (NELF) indicates the attorney has actually practiced law related to health and long-term care planning; public benefits (such as Medicaid, Medicare, and Social Security); surrogate decision-making (for example, powers of attorney and guardianship); older persons' legal capacity; and the conservation, disposition, and administration of the older person's estate (includes wills, trust and probate of an estate). Some states also have their own certification programs for these specialities.

Financial planners provide comprehensive financial and personal asset management, including debt, income, asset, insurance, tax, investment, and net worth analysis. They can help establish priorities; advise about paying for your child's education, planning for a disabled child's care, retirement planning, buying or selling a business, and managing the financial impact of other major life events; develop a plan for growing wealth; and counsel on which financial products and services best suit your needs. Look for someone who has achieved one of the following designations: Chartered Financial Analyst (CFA) offered by the Association of Investment Management and Research; Certified Financial Planner (CFP), offered by the Certified Financial Planner Board of Standards, Inc.; or Chartered Financial Consultant (ChFC), offered by American College in Bryn Mawr, Pennsylvania. These designations are awarded based on slightly different criteria — courses and tests — but any one of them demonstrates the practitioner's commitment to becoming a financial expert and to continuing education in the field. Beyond that, you'll want to interview them to learn more about whether their personality suits your own and to discover what their individual preference is — whether they prefer general financial planning, accounting, or more specialized investment planning, as the case may be.

Insurance brokers sell insurance products that can form the basis of an estate, safeguard your assets, provide income, pay for long-term and health care, and provide liquidity so bills can be paid prior to estate settlement. Insurance brokers must have a state-issued license. Those who wish to sell mutual funds and variable annuities must pass a licensing exam administered by the National Association of Securities Dealers (NASD).

Insurance companies themselves are rated for financial stability by the following independent organizations: A.M. Best Company (www.ambest.com), Moody's Investors Service (www.moodys.com), and Standard & Poor's (www.standardandpoors.com). If you are buying insurance from a company, you'll want to look for a stable company, such as one that has an A++, A+ (Superior) rating from A.M. Best.

Investment advisors provide information about stocks, bonds, and other investment vehicles to grow your money. In order to buy and sell securities, the broker must have licenses and passed exams by the National Association of Securities Dealers (NASD) or the Financial Industry Regulatory Authority (FINRA). Licensing typically requires employment with a company.

The Role of Financial Planning in Estate Planning

Estate-planning professionals may have different perspectives and different kinds of expertise, but they all typically have one thing in common: a financial background. You might think of estate and financial planning as two wheels on the same bike, connected but separate, yet still moving in tandem. Some parts of estate planning, such as health care decision-making, taking a personal property inventory, or proving an individual's mental competency, have little to do with money, but in planning for your future and the future of your loved ones — which is what estate planning is all about — the advantages of financial planning cannot be overlooked.

A financial plan provides a solid foundation for any estate plan. By managing your money well, the likelihood is that you'll enjoy more years of good health because you will feel less distressed about finances, be able to take care of yourself, and able pay for necessary care and assistance with activities of daily living as you get older. You'll be able to enjoy a stable, comfortable home environment, through strategic management of your finances. Not only will you be able to pay for the roof over your head but create income to pay for ongoing expenses. Sound financial management allows you to grow wealth that can continue to provide for those you love and the causes you believe in after you're long gone. Such wealth can be transferred through wills, trusts, and certain other financial documents and can be managed by your powers of attorney.

Comprehensive estate planning also utilizes financial planning to help create options for your future when you retire or are no longer able to work due to disability or other personal circumstances, need assistance with the tasks of daily living, or require expensive medical care. In addition, estate planning utilizes financial instruments to help you manage your assets, reducing tax liability and protecting and preserving them so you have something to pass on. A financial advisor may not help you write a will or draft a trust instrument, but he or she may help you manage, accumulate, invest and ultimately, grow the money that will be assigned through those legal documents. As you can see, estate planning and financial planning overlap a good deal.

Working with a Financial Planner

Trying to learn everything there is to know about the financial aspects of estate planning can be overwhelming, so it makes sense to start the process by setting some priorities. Your finances and how you manage them (or don't) reflect not only who you are, but the circumstances you find yourself in. If you have many years ahead in which to save for retirement, or are childless, you may have very different priorities and a different willingness to take more risk with your investments and your plans than someone who is older and who has children or is supporting someone who is disabled. It's best, therefore, to consult with a financial professional who knows the ins and outs of estate planning.

Many people with few assets hesitate to consult with a financial planner. That's a mistake. Financial planning is not for the rich alone. In fact, it may be even more important for those who have just a few assets and tiny estates to work with an expert to *grow* their money. After all, what is a thousand dollars here or there to someone who leaves a million-dollar estate? Only a tiny percentage of the estate. But if your resources are slim, a thousand dollars represents a far greater percentage of your estate. The more modest the resources, the more care one should take. Many experts point out that if people are without assets it's not because they don't earn a high income, but, rather, because they don't understand *how to* make the most of what they have. It's not what you bring home, but what you do with it that counts. It is well worth it, they say, to spend a couple of hundred dollars to sit down for an hour with an expert for advice.

There are also organizations you can join that provide advice on financial-planning matters, either through telephone help lines or newsletters. Community colleges often offer courses on financial planning for the cost of a couple of visits to a fast-food restaurant, and some social services agencies or consumer credit counseling services can help you with your finances as well.

But probably the biggest obstacle to financial planning is simply mindset. Ironically, the idea of having enough money to afford a financial planner is relative. I have known individuals who have earned well above six-figures for decades but who thought themselves too poor to afford a financial planner. When they finally sat down and spoke to one, they learned in the space of fifteen minutes how they could have saved themselves more than $10,000 a year for the past two decades. Even with a conservative investment return (unlike the higher returns of the last two decades), that money would be worth several hundreds of thousands of dollars today. That fifteen minutes of the financial planner's time cost this couple $50. They are certainly glad to have the advice now, but they can't help regret the money they lost out on because they were reluctant to spend a lesser sum twenty years ago.

In the best of all possible worlds, your financial plan and your estate plan will work seamlessly together and grow and change as your needs and circumstances do. Both your financial and your estate plan should therefore be periodically adjusted in light of your goals and your progress towards them. An annual review of your estate plans and supporting financial and legal documents is highly recommended, in addition to a review after any major life change, such as marriage, divorce, or the birth of a child, or a change in the laws.

MAKING A PLAN

Whether you are just beginning to think long-term and hope to better manage your finances, or you're already prepared for retirement and are worried about distributing an estate once you're gone, you'll need an estate plan. The following list of questions is designed to help you create one.

Estate-Planning Checklist

❏ What do I want to accomplish?

❏ What would my goal look like if it were implemented?

❏ What information do I need to make a plan/decision?

❏ What resources (funding, people) can help me accomplish my goal?

❏ What options do I think I have?

❏ What do professional advisors recommend?

❏ Reviewing my options, and taking professional advice, personal inclination, and the factors listed above into account, what plan looks like it is best suited to helping me reach my goal?

❏ What steps do I need to take to implement my plan? (Include a deadline for implementing each step.)

❏ Discuss the plan with affected parties.

❏ Monitor the plan annually (or more often if necessary).

—From the Expert—————————————

Attorney David Posner on the fundamentals of estate planning

An attorney with Morrison, Posner & Kramer, L.L.P. in Millburn, New Jersey (www.posnerkramer.com), David Posner specializes in estate planning and elder law. His numerous credentials include membership in the New Jersey State Bar Association Real Property, Probate and Trust, and Elder Law Sections and the American Bar Association Probate and Trust section, the American Health Lawyers Association, Estate Planning Council of Northern New Jersey, Inc., and National Academy of Elder Law Attorneys. Mr. Posner is also the former President and Secretary of the New Jersey Society of Hospital Attorneys. He has lectured for the New Jersey Graduate Program in Public Health, University of Medicine and Dentistry of New Jersey at Rutgers, and the State University of New Jersey. Below, he shares some of his insights about estate planning, starting with the importance of having legal documents in place so that your loved ones can make appropriate financial and medical decisions for you if you become unable to do so.

- **People often get confused between the term "will" and "living will."** An easy way to remember the difference is: a will *is not* effective until you die. The other three important estate-planning documents — the power of attorney, advance directive, and living will — are *only* effective until you die.

- **You absolutely should have a power of attorney, even if you think you've got a long life ahead of you.** You could become laid up with an illness for weeks, and someone's got to have access to your assets to pay the mortgage, the utility bills, real estate tax — all of the things that the average person has to pay.

- **It is so important for people to have a medical power of attorney and living will so others know what their intentions are, and to let family members know that they've signed such documents.** Even if you have a living will, problems can arise in implementing it. I was on the bioethics committee of a hospital. Sometimes there can be a conflict between how the doctors want to treat a patient and how the patient wants to be treated. If you have a living will, your health care representative or family can take it to the bioethics committee if there is such a conflict. The truth is, sometimes the patient or the patient's family has got to stand up for the patient's rights.

- **Some people don't like to appoint someone outside of a spouse as power of attorney because they are afraid that people will use it before it's necessary and leave the patient out of the discussion, so they'll leave the document with the attorney.** Any requests for the document must then come to the attorney; he or she will act as a kind of gatekeeper for the document.

- **The situation of a colleague of mine demonstrates what happens when people don't review their will periodically and whenever a major life event occurs.** My colleague was married and without children. He drafted his own will and left his estate to his wife. He put his funeral arrangements in the will. His wife died, but he never changed the terms of his will. By the laws of the state, his nieces and nephews, as beneficiaries and next-of-kin, were responsible for paying for his burial. The funeral home wanted all of them to sign off on the funeral arrangements. We didn't even know where they all lived. My colleague had also neglected to leave a list with their names and addresses.

- **People often do estate planning, but they never review the beneficiaries of their life insurance or benefits plans to make sure that they reflect their estate plan.** If they want to name someone as the beneficiary of an insurance policy and then name someone else as the beneficiary of the estate passed through the will, that's fine, but often I find that the opposite is true — they end up with a will that leaves their total estate to one person, and a life insurance policy that names someone else as the beneficiary, even when their plan was to leave the estate to the same person. In our firm, we make a point of filling out all of the beneficiary forms for the life insurance policies, 401(k) plans, IRAs, and so on, on our client's behalf, at the time that we draft the will, so we are sure the beneficiary designation plans follow their estate plans

- **Word-of-mouth from a trusted source is one of the best ways to find an attorney.** Sometimes people will attend seminars put on by attorneys, but just because someone runs a seminar doesn't mean what they are saying is correct. For example, in New Jersey, an attorney was putting on a seminar trying to convince people they needed a revocable ("living") trust. In Florida, when you die, the state requires that you prepare a list of assets, which then must be inventoried as part of the estate; this costs money. Transferring your assets to a revocable trust in this instance can help avoid some of the probate expense. In New Jersey, however, you are not required to produce a real property inventory, so this reason for transferring your assets to a revocable trust doesn't exist.

- **One situation where a revocable trust may come in handy, however, is a case where someone owns property in different states.**

For example, suppose someone lives in Pennsylvania but has a house at the Jersey Shore. Without using an estate-planning tool, such as transferring the property to a trust or a Limited Liability Corporation (LLC), the estate will have to be probated in both states, which increases costs.

- I often get clients, especially older women, who have pages and pages of things they want to leave to people, and they want to include these pages in the will. If they do incorporate them in the will, it becomes part of the estate return, and now it must be inventoried and appraised, which is an expense. In New Jersey, you don't need to include this inventory in the will. By statute, you can leave personal property to people in a handwritten letter, and this reduces costs.

- **There are people who like to rule from the grave, which I think is a mistake.** Outside of protecting the interests of a disabled dependent or managing for someone who has an addiction that precludes them from being able to manage their affairs, in the ordinary course of events, it's best to leave people to lead their own lives. I have a client in his nineties who has two twin daughters that he wanted to leave a substantial portion of his estate to. One of them got married in her late fifties to a man the father did not like. He was concerned the husband would come to his daughter and ask her for substantial sums of money to pay large debts. He wanted to put the money in a trust and to include a statement that the trust would terminate and his daughter would get all of the money if she divorced her husband. But that's actively encouraging divorce. So, instead, we put it in a trust for her until she's seventy-five. She'll get the income from it until that age, at which time the remaining money will be transferred to her. It's unlikely that her husband, who is older than she is, will still be alive at that point.

YOUR FINANCIAL OVERVIEW

The following documents provide the foundation for your financial plan and, ultimately, your estate plan. These are the documents that lay out what your present financial state is. They are critical to putting all of your money to work for you. They provide your financial advisor with a baseline of necessary information to enable him or her to formulate action steps to help you manage your current assets, protecting what you have, and helping you enhance your estate in the years ahead. They also give your attorney the information needed to draft other documents that can help you to shelter your assets and transfer them at death to your loved ones or other beneficiaries that you designate. Whether your estate is small or large, whether you are up to your ears in debt and struggling financially or have amassed a nice nest egg, these documents are critical to understanding where you are now — and where you want to be in the future.

- Income Statement
- Asset Inventory
- Expense Statement
- Liability Statement
- Net Worth Statement
- Other documents that might contribute to your financial well-being

Income Statement

An income statement is an essential tool for achieving your savings goals for retirement, education of minor children, and wealth accumulation. Start by creating a list of all of your consistent sources of income, including all side businesses, such as selling goods on ebay or hobbies that generate cash. At a high level, you'll include the dollars you get from your:

- Salary
- Interest and dividends from savings and other financial instruments, such as annuities and trusts
- Investment dividends and income
- Child support
- Alimony

- Real estate rental income
- Internet Web site income
- Home or small business income
- Freelance work
- Gifts of money
- Social Security

- Pension benefits
- IRA
- 401(k)s
- Royalties on intellectual property
- Hobbies

You'll use this income statement to calculate your net worth statement, which is essential to understanding the value of your estate. But before we get to that, you'll need to do something else: calculate your expense statement.

Expense Statement

List all of your expenses. If you already have a budget — or "spending plan," as some prefer to call it — that you live by, you're one step ahead! Your financial advisor — or the individual appointed to keep things running if you become incapacitated — will appreciate not having to play archeologist. If not, you'll need to create one. The expense statement is most helpful if it provides an overview of your monthly outlay, any periodic large payments you make, as well as a comprehensive overview of the annual costs that you incur to maintain your present lifestyle. *(When you need to pay your bills is as important as how much the bills are.)*

Your financial advisor may be able to suggest ways to save and juggle payments that can help you not only avoid incurring additional expenses in the form of interest payments, but which may actually earn you interest as well. The list should detail the due dates of, and amounts associated with, such bills as:

- Housing (rent or mortgage) payments
- Home equity loans and lines of credit
- Other loans

- Real estate taxes
- Insurance, including life, health, and home
- Utilities (heat, electricity, water, sewer, garbage)

- Credit card balances and payments
- Real estate taxes
- Car payments or other fixed transportation costs

- Vet bills
- Phone bills

Flexible expenses should be detailed separately from fixed expenses, so you can understand how much money you have to work with outside of paying for basic necessities. Samples of flexible expenses include:

- Home maintenance
- Auto maintenance
- Gas
- Food
- Personal grooming
- Clothing
- Gifts
- Dining out
- Entertainment

- Cable TV
- Fitness club
- Hobbies
- Clubs
- Travel
- Education costs (unless you are currently a full-time student)
- Sports and other recreation

Asset Inventory

Beyond income, your net worth is also derived from other assets, for example, things that you own. This can include material goods — such as the house you live in and the items it's furnished with — and intellectual property, such as any patents or copyrights you might own. At a high level, your assets statement should list things like:

- Bank, investment, retirement, savings account balances
- Intellectual property (patents, copyrights, trademarks)

- The estimated value of your house
- The value of any real property you own, including:
    - Automobiles
    - Furniture and home furnishings
    - Jewelry
    - Electronic equipment
    - Antiques

(For more details on real property, see Chapter 3.)

Liability Statement

Your liabilities are, simply put, the sum total of any costs owed. How is a liability different from an expense? For example, your expense statement details your monthly outlay on your mortgage, but your liability statement identifies what the balance of the unpaid mortgage — what you still owe on that mortgage — is. Let's say your monthly mortgage is $1,500 but you still owe $200,000 on your house. If you should die, the monthly expense will be helpful in determining the cost to the estate to keep things running until the estate settles. So, $1,500 goes on your expense statement. The liability statement, on the other hand, is used to determine the expenses that need to be subtracted from the estate to determine its actual monetary value. For example, the $200,000 balance on the mortgage is a liability that must be subtracted from the overall worth of the estate to determine the actual estate value. The mortgage will have to be satisfied prior to the final distribution of the estate's assets. If the house isn't passing to a beneficiary, administrators sometimes allow for a partial or incremental distribution of assets (depending on the size of the estate), holding up the final distribution until the house is sold. Other liabilities might include outstanding balances on your mortgage and home equity loans, credit cards, automobile loans, student loans, and other obligations.

Your Net Worth Statement

Another reason for doing your homework creating asset and liability statements and so on is to create a net worth statement. The net worth statement is created by subtracting your liabilities from your assets. Compiled annually, your net worth statement acts as a measurement tool for charting your progress towards your broader financial goals and helps your financial advisor determine the best way to advise you on reaching those goals.

The Net Worth Formula

Assets $_____ - Liabilities $_____ = Net worth $ _____

ESTATE ADMINISTRATION

The various documents that you've prepared as part of your estate plan all play a part when it comes to administering your estate. Although there are some differences between the different states, and depending on the deceased's circumstances, the checklist below provides an overview of the steps that are typically involved in an ordinary estate settlement:

❑ The estate is formally opened in probate court.

❑ A personal representative for the estate is appointed and approved by the court. Usually the personal representative is named in the will. However, even though the deceased has named a personal representative, that individual still must accept the appointment and the court must approve it. Because the personal representative has a fiduciary responsibility, he or she may be required to post a bond if the deceased has not waived this requirement in the will.

❑ Estate assets are collected, inventoried, and valued. This may require hiring appraisers if the assets are collectibles, antiques, or other items that have significant value.

❑ The personal representative continues to oversee the management of estate assets, such as real estate and investments, in order to preserve the value of the estate, until such time as the assets are distributed.

❑ A notice to creditors that the estate is open is published in the newspaper, so they can file any outstanding claims against the estate. Usually (but check state law to be sure) claims must be presented within six months to be honored; this deadline enables the estate to be settled relatively quickly.

❑ The personal representative files any required tax returns. This may include federal estate tax and income tax returns, a state death tax, and any other of the deceased's personal tax returns not filed prior to death.

❑ Debts are paid.

❑ Property, if any, may be sold according to the laws of the state and the will.

❑ A final accounting is submitted to the probate court, which reviews it. Once the court is satisfied that everything is in order, it will authorize final distribution of the estate's assets.

❑ The remainder of the estate — the "net" after deduction of all costs and expenses — is distributed to the beneficiaries as designated by the will.

❑ The personal representative petitions the court to be discharged from his or her duties and responsibilities.

❑ If the court approves, the estate is formally settled.

RESOURCES

ELDER LAW, ESTATE-PLANNING ATTORNEYS, AND LEGAL ASSISTANCE

American Bar Association
740 15th Street, N.W., Washington D.C. 20005-1022
Phone: 202-662-8690; Fax: 202-662-8698
Web site: www.abanet.org/aging

Estateplanninglinks.com
Phone: 877-909-1122
Web site: www.estateplanninglinks.com

LawHelp
Web site: www.lawhelp.org

National Academy of Elder Law Attorneys (NAELA™)
1604 North Country Club Road, Tucson, AZ 85716
Phone: 520-881-4005; Fax: 520-325-7925
Web site: www.naela.org

National Bar Association (NBA)
1225 11th Street, NW, Washington, D.C. 20001
Phone: 202-842-3900; Fax: 202-289-6170
Web site: www.nationalbar.org (Click on "Resources" link.)

National Senior Citizens Law Center (NSCLC)
1101 14th Street, NW, Suite 400, Washington, D.C. 20005
Phone: 202-289-6976; Fax: 202-289-7224
Web site: www.nsclc.org

Pro Seniors (State Legal Hotlines for Seniors)
Web site: http:///www.proseniors.org/National_Hotline_List.html

FINANCIAL AND ESTATE PLANNING

The American Institute of Certified Public Accountants (AICPA®)
1211 Avenue of the Americas, New York, NY 10036
Web site: www.aicpa.org; also sponsors two unique Web sites to help people with money management: www.feedthepig.org and www.360financialliteracy.org

Certified Financial Planner Board of Standards, Inc.
1670 Broadway, Suite 600, Denver, CO 80202
Web site: www.cfp.net

Choose to Save®
1100 13th St. NW, Suite 878, Washington, D.C. 20005-4204
Phone: 202-659-0670; Fax: 202-775-6312
Web site: www.choosetosave.org

Federal Citizen Information Service
Phone: 888-878-3256
Web site: www.pueblo.gsa.gov

Financial Industry Regulatory Authority (FINRA)
1735 K St. NW, Washington, DC 20006
Web site: www.finra.org

Financial Planning Association® (FPA®)
4100 E. Mississippi Ave., Suite 400, Denver, CO 80246-3053
Web site: www.fpanet.org

Financial Security Later in Life (USDA web page)
Web site: www.csrees.usda.gov/nea/economics/fsll/fsll.html

MetLife Mature Market Institute®
Web site: www.maturemarketinstitute.com

MyMoney.gov by the U.S. Financial Literacy and Education Commission
Phone: 888-MYMONEY
Web site: www.mymoney.gov

National Association of Estate Planners & Councils
1120 Chester Avenue, Suite 470, Cleveland, OH 44114
Phone: 866-226-2224; Fax: 216-696-2582
Web site: www.naepc.org

National Committee on Planned Giving®
233 McCrea Street, Suite 400, Indianapolis, IN 46225
Phone: 317-269-6274; Fax: 317-269-6276
Web site: www.ncpg.org

National Consumer's League (NCL)
1701 K Street, NW, Suite 1200, Washington DC 20006
Phone: 202-835-3323; Fax: 202-835-0747
Web site: www.nclnet.org

Pension Rights Center (PRC)
1350 Connecticut Ave. NW, Suite 206, Washington DC 20036
Phone: 202-296-3776; Fax: 202-833-2472
Web site: www.pensionrights.org

NOTES

Chapter 3:
Real Estate, Real Property, and Other Illiquid Assets

MY DOCUMENTS AT-A-GLANCE

Fill in the chart below to keep track of where your critical documents will be stored and who will have access to them.

DOCUMENT	LOCATION	ACCESS/COPY GIVEN TO
Automobile title		
Automobile repair records		
Budget or household account book		
Coins or other valuable items		
Durable power of attorney (real estate)		
Household inventory		
Insurance		
Jewelry		
Lease		
Mortgage/real estate lien documents		

My Documents at-a-Glance (continued)

DOCUMENT	LOCATION	ACCESS/COPY GIVEN TO
Motor vehicle registration		
Photographs		
Real estate deeds, settlement documents, etc.		
Real estate receipts and other records		
Real property inventory		
Tax documents (real estate)		
Warranties (products)		
Other		

ASSET OWNERSHIP

The last chapter established that an essential part of estate planning is identifying your assets and and creating a comprehensive estate plan. You also learned that one of the key steps in settling an estate is figuring out the best way to transfer your assets to beneficiaries, either as part of the probate process (typically through a will) or outside of the probate process, through a trust or other means of transfer, such as assigning or gifting assets to someone beforehand. Finally, you learned that a key job of an estate's administrator is to make an accounting of your assets and ensure they are disposed of properly according to the laws of the state that the estate is being probated in. We also talked about the importance of financial planning and evaluating your financial assets. Because an understanding of asset ownership is so important to estate planning and administration, we'll continue to talk more about it in this chapter. You'll begin by learning about two special kinds of assets almost everybody owns. Next, we'll discuss real property assets, which have a major impact on the estate process.

Two Kinds of Assets

Assets are typically divided into two categories: liquid and illiquid assets. *Liquid assets* are the kinds of things you can easily access, turn into cash, and dispose of quickly — stocks, bonds, and cash, for example. As long as an individual is authorized to access an account, he or she can sell a stock or transfer funds from a bank account relatively quickly. Today, with online banking, a simple click of a button is all it takes (although settlement of actual funds may take a few more days).

Illiquid assets are more difficult and time-consuming to turn into cash. Examples of illiquid assets are real estate, including the house you live in; personal property, such as your home's furnishings and furniture; any other material goods that you own, such as artwork, collectibles, or vehicles; and *business equity,* which includes any business(es) and related business assets that you may own, in whole or in part. Disposing of these items usually is an involved process, consisting of identifying or inventorying the assets, establishing ownership, assigning a value to them, finding a buyer for them or putting them up for sale or auction, and, finally, collecting and distributing the cash proceeds from the sale. As you can imagine, all together, these activities can take a substantial amount of time and sometimes require the assistance of specialists, such as auction houses or business valuation and brokering services. The economy can weigh in, too; for example, trying to sell a house in a down market may take a long time. Depending on the complexity involved with assigning a value to an asset and selling it, turning it into cash could take months, years, even decades, which is why such assets are considered *illiquid.*

Despite the difficulties involved in disposing of them, illiquid assets play a significant role in financial planning, wealth management, and estate planning. According to the Federal Reserve, which periodically reports on family finances, the largest share of the American family's total assets — slightly more than 64% in 2004 — consists of non-financial assets. The primary residence made up the largest share (more than half) of these non-financial assets, a figure borne out by the Federal Deposit Insurance Corporation (FDIC), which every few years issues a report on consumer finances. It quotes data from a 2006 Federal Reserve bulletin that reveals the single largest source of wealth for retirees is often their primary residence. So it's important when organizing your affairs to understand the process of disposing of real property and which documents need to be available in order to make property transfers go as smoothly as possible.

THE PROPERTY INVENTORY

The first step in disposing of real property assets is to identify them. As with financial assets, you can do this with an up-to-date inventory, listing any real property assets you own. The person who's settling your estate will need to know what you own, where it's physically located, and how to access it, as well as the location of any important documents describing the item and establishing clear ownership and value. You should also consider making notes alongside each item on the inventory list about how you'd like the assets listed to be handled upon your death. Finally, take a photograph of each item (or at least the most important ones) to accompany the inventory list.

Depending on your situation, you may need more than one inventory to capture different types of property characteristics and meet the specific record-keeping requirements of each. For example:

• **Real estate inventory:** In addition to the location of any residential or commercial properties owned and a legal description of them (this typically includes the county and township in which the property is located, along with its deed and parcel ID numbers, lot dimensions, and boundaries), provide its estimated fair market value, plus information about any mortgages and liens, as well as the location of important papers such as deeds, titles, sale agreements, leases or other contracts, tenant application and contact information, insurance policies, and tax information.

• **Personal property inventory:** This covers the contents of your home or other building, such as a garage, boathouse, stable, or storage facility. Typical items found on an inventory list are: furniture; decorative objects and accessories; soft furnishings, such as curtains, carpets, pillows, and bedspreads; personal clothing and items, including jewelry; equipment and appliances; and automobiles, boats, and other vehicles. An easy and effective way to inventory a building is to go through it one room at a time (kitchen, bathroom, dining room, bedroom, etc.), noting the items contained in each room together with any relevant details, such as:

- *the condition it's in*

- *where it was purchased*

- *brand name*

- *model number*

- *serial number*

- *date purchased*

- *purchase cost*

- *replacement cost*

- *serial number or other ID number*

- *warranty information*

- *for automobiles, you'll need to provide IDs from proof of ownership and registration documents, including registration and VIN numbers, and where to find the title.*

Along with recording items on a household inventory list, you should keep receipts to prove the cost; to file an insurance claim, you typically need to know how much it would cost to replace each item. Photograph each room and the items on the inventory list with a digital camera (be sure to mark the photos with the corresponding inventory control number) and store the pictures with the inventory list in a safety deposit box.

The room-by-room approach also helps executors of an estate, who are not always familiar with everything you own and where you keep it, to find certain items that may have been mentioned in the will or that need to be evaluated by auctioneers or estate sales firms.

• **Antiques or collectibles inventory:** If you are a connoisseur of wine, a collector of coins, stamps, art, antique cars, furniture, or some other type of collectible, you'll want to create a separate collection inventory. This should contain a description of the item, where and when it was purchased and from whom, any notes about provenance or attributes that add to the collectible's value, and any information that would point to recent market prices, including insurance policies and what it's currently insured for, and possible dealers or collectors it could be sold to if you don't intend to pass them on to a specific beneficiary

• **Business assets inventory:** Depending on the type and size of the business, this kind of asset inventory can be quite complex, encompassing both liquid and illiquid assets, including financial assets, real estate and real property assets, intellectual property assets, and so on. Be sure to include important supporting documents in the asset inventory file, such as contracts, partnership agreements and articles of incorporation, business plans, account books, with records of equipment purchases and leases, assets, expenses, receivables, sales, property leases or deeds, certificates, and licenses. For the purposes of your estate plan, be sure to identify your share of ownership in the business's assets and note any contractual obligations that may affect asset ownership, distribution, or transfer.

You may want to consider contracting with a professional who specializes in this type of work. Look for estate inventory specialists, appraisers, and auctioneers in your phone directory or see the Resources section at the end of this chapter for more information. A third-party appraisal can often aid the estate process by providing an unbiased assessment of an item or property's worth, lending legitimacy to the inventory and ensuring its completeness. In addition, appraisals are often required in certain circumstances, such as when an item is going to an auction house for disposal. Whether you decide to hire a professional, or leave it to your personal representative to manage the inventory and pay someone to do it from estate proceeds, if you prepare your own detailed inventory you'll help to reduce costs by cutting down on the time it takes to identify and assemble everything — little or big — that you have accumulated over the course of your lifetime.

Titling Your Assets

Whether recorded on your asset inventory or elsewhere, it's extremely important that you provide your estate professionals and personal representative with information and documentation about asset ownership. Do you own the property or your car outright? Or will someone else need to sign an agreement to sell it? Many times people don't understand that the type of ownership affects how property is passed at death. The three common types of property ownership are:

• **By individual name:** Your name is listed by itself on a title, deed, or contract. When you die, these assets will be used to pay any debts and then they will be distributed to your beneficiaries as part of the probate process. Because the probate process is usually controlled by county or state law, the beneficiaries will be chosen by the probate court unless you have a valid will identifying your chosen beneficiaries.

• **Jointly:** More than one person is listed as the property owner on a title, deed, or contract. Property may be jointly owned by *tenants with rights of survivorship*, in which case, if one of the owners listed on the contract dies, ownership of the property remains with the surviving joint tenants, and so ownership passes outside of the probate process. On the other hand, if the property is owned jointly by *tenants-in-common,* when one of the owners dies, his or her portion of the property is treated as if it were owned in the *individual's* name. The individual can then leave it to a beneficiary in a will, in which case it passes through the probate process. A *tenancy by the entirety* is a type of ownership in which a husband and wife both have right to the entire property. Upon the death of one spouse, title passes to the other (*right of survivorship*).

• **By contract/agreement:** A contract has been made and signed between an individual and a third party, such as an employer, insurance broker, bank, etc., designating one or more persons who are to receive the asset upon the individual's death. For example, you may name a beneficiary to an insurance policy, retirement plan, or trust agreement (a trust may own a physical property, such as a house). The asset is then transferred — that is, in the case of property, distributed — to the beneficiary upon the individual's death without having to go through the probate process.

One of most common mistakes made in estate planning is not paying attention to how assets are titled. If you do not own assets as an individual, they will not pass through your will. While this can be a benefit, it also can be a negative if the way the assets are titled prevents your estate plan from being carried out. For example, suppose you had a son and daughter, and you want to provide for them in your estate equally. But at some point, you need help managing your affairs, and so you name your son as a joint tenant on all of your assets. When you die, even though your will says your estate is to be equally divided between the two children, your daughter will inherit nothing, because her brother already owns the assets. If you name your daughter as the beneficiary of a life insurance policy, that, too, would pass outside of the will (that is, outside of the probate process), so the money in the life insurance policy would not pass to the son, even though your will states your assets are to be "equally divided."

Since real property in the name of husband and wife automatically passes to the surviving spouse, a man who willed his Corvette to his nephew would certainly be surprised to find his wife driving it around town because real property in the name of husband and wife automatically passes to the surviving spouse. The widow who forgot to remove her husband as beneficiary on her 401(k) program might be surprised to learn that her second husband will get the money in it rather than the children from the first marriage that she willed 100% of her estate to. Even if family members in such scenarios would be willing to return money from assets passed outside of probate, they most likely would be subject to a penalty in the form of a gift tax. That's why it's critical to review all of your assets with your attorney at the time the will is drafted, and to pay special attention to ownership and beneficiary designations when creating an estate plan.

Assigning a Value to Your Assets

We've hinted at the benefit of using a professional appraiser to review your asset inventory so that an appropriate reserve can be set or an estimated price can be provided for assets sold at auction. But even if you think that the items you own aren't worth fixing a price to, you should attempt to place some value on them. If they are passed through probate, most likely the estate will require that a value be assigned to them for the purpose of determining how much your estate is worth — and whether and how much it can be taxed. If you plan to distribute items equitably to family members or beneficiaries outside of probate, you may be able to forestall arguments that someone got something worth more than somebody else by assigning a value to each item on the inventory, writing the amount alongside the asset and the name of the person you're leaving it to. If you decide to get rid of the asset yourself as part of getting your affairs in order, you may want to keep a record of the value of any item donated to a charity's thrift shop so that you can write it off your personal taxes. In fact, the Salvation Army and many other non-profit charitable organizations have price lists that you can use to assign a value to a household item for this very purpose.

Detailed property records and household inventories are also essential estate-planning documents in themselves, helping your financial planner to advise you on asset allocation, your attorney to determine what will — and what will not — pass through probate, and your insurance agent to suggest the amount and type of coverage you should have. (Added benefits include supporting your insurance claim filings if you experience a flood, hurricane, earthquake, fire, or other disaster, documenting your losses for tax purposes, and providing proof of ownership in case of a divorce or separation.) In sum, they are invaluable when it comes to assessing the size of your estate and providing your panel of professional advisors with the information they need in order to advise you on the best way to structure your estate plan.

Distribution of Personal Property

Once you've inventoried your assets and established how you own them, it's time to give thought to the individuals (or even charities) you'd like to give them to and how ownership should be transferred. In your will you can bequeath a specific dollar amount, asset, or piece of property or a percentage of the estate that remains after all debts have been satisfied and expenses, including taxes and administration costs, have been paid. Naturally, you'll want to get input from your team of professional advisors — and your attorney in particular. But before doing so, you might want to make some notes about how you'd like to dispose of these assets. This will help your attorney to understand your intent. If a decision is made that the items need not be passed through a will, and your state allows for it, you may decide to direct the distribution of real property assets in a letter.

ASSET INVENTORY

The chart below will help you identify the details of assets you'd like to pass on to others.

ITEM	DESCRIPTION	LOCATION	ESTIMATED VALUE	BENEFICIARY

—From the Expert—

Real estate broker Diane Turner Valeri on being savvy about your property

Diane Turner Valeri, a real estate broker with Weichert Realty in New Jersey, has worked with many older individuals as they seek to downsize or sell estate property. Here are some of her words of wisdom:

- If you are putting your affairs in order to help smooth the transition for those taking control of your estate, you'll have to give some thought to selling your property at some point or transferring it to someone else before or after your death. **There are three real estate-related documents that I think you'd want to find and keep close at hand: the deed, the survey, and the title policy for your property.** From these three documents you can get almost everything you need to sell or assign the property.

- **The deed is important to keep on hand because proving clear title is important; any liens or other encumbrances can make property difficult to sell.** Although it's recorded and can be found in the county office, having the deed on hand will save time and effort in the search.

- **The survey will show you what the property actually consists of, and, in addition, it will show any setbacks, wells, septic systems, and outbuildings.** Many times a potential buyer looks at a property and wants to make some changes — put on an addition, install an in-ground swimming pool or fence. If you have a survey, you can find out almost immediately what the options are and whether there's any environmental hazard, such as an abandoned in-ground oil tank. For example, you might discover that the place where you wanted to install a pool is already occupied by a septic tank. The survey isn't typically recorded, so it's important that you keep a copy. Sometimes property lines aren't clear, especially on older properties, and issues need to be resolved. There have actually been cases where houses were built on property that the people building the house thought they owned but didn't. Surveys need to be within the last seven years to be considered current.

- **Title insurance insures the quality of your ownership.** If you have the title papers, then any new title search will only have to go as far back as your ownership.

- Many times people keep a pile of papers related to the purchase of a home in their attic, and then they have to go sorting through boxes to find the critical documents. **Especially in a competitive market, you or your heirs will want to avoid keeping an empty house on the market for any length of time, so this information will need to be accessible, because buyers can be impatient.**

- **Another important document is any letter regarding a financial hazard, such as an abandoned well, septic tank, or fuel tank, stating that the item was properly disposed of.** You can lose a buyer if there is any question of an environmental issue with the property or feature, such as an abandoned, filled-in swimming pool that limits the property's value.

- **Another big issue that comes up with estates is the clean-out.** As you get your affairs in order, do as much of the clean-out yourself as possible. Often this is very difficult for the older person, who may have grown up in a poor household and learned to save everything because it might come in handy some day. And people do tend to get emotionally bonded to stuff, even stuff that isn't very usable or attractive. If you're moving to an assisted living facility, the move will be a catalyst, because, chances are, you won't be able to take everything with you. You can look at the clean-up as a new beginning, or a chance to help someone else out.

- **Giving mementos is a really nice way to size down.** My mother went through all of these family photos and sent them off to the relatives that would most appreciate them. She got a lot of nice letters from all of the people she sent them to, saying how much they appreciated her doing that. Another nice way to size down is to give things away to charity. It's important for younger people and family members to realize that many of the things they regard as junk may have precious associations and meaning to others or could benefit those in need. So practice saying, "Wouldn't so-and-so just love this?" or "I'll bet this dining set would really help the battered women's shelter . . ." or "Wouldn't these clothes be perfect for the church bazaar?"

- Many times people prefer to spend their final years in their own home, in the familiar neighborhood surrounded by neighbors and friends. **If you are planning to stay in your house for some time — or forever — give some thought to modernizing it.** Update the kitchen, put in that new bathroom you've been thinking about. Update the electric and plumbing. And while you're at it, make it easier for living. Put in a self-cleaning oven. Light the dark basement steps. Put in energy-saving fixtures, water heaters, and appliances. You'll get to enjoy the easier lifestyle and the savings on your utilities, and when it comes time to sell the house, it will be more salable and will profit everybody.

- **People get overwhelmed when they don't stick to a plan of doing at least one improvement project a year.** The more time goes by, the more the projects close in. Then everything tends to happen at once: the roof leaks, the plumbing leaks, and you need a new furnace all at the same time.

- **Think out of the box.** One of my clients did what I think was a clever thing. Her property was getting a bit much for her to handle by herself, so she started looking at condos. When she realized she would have to pay a monthly maintenance fee of a few hundred dollars, she decided to go a different route. She found a home handyman and paid him the $300 a month "on retainer" to take care of her house. That way she was able to stay in her home.

Legal Look: Reverse Mortgages

Reverse mortgages offer older adults a way to draw on the equity they've built up in their homes without having to sell them or meet income guidelines and make the monthly payments typically required by a standard home equity loan or line of credit. The more equity you have in your house, the bigger your reverse mortgage can be. Interest rates and your age are also a factor in calculating how much you can get. You can receive the money in a lump sum, or as needed, or in regular payments. You won't have to pay back the reverse mortgage for as long as you live in your house, but the loan amount cannot exceed the value of the home at the time it's repaid — when the last borrower dies, sells the home, or moves. As the owner, you still have to maintain your home, pay taxes on it, and make insurance payments.

At the date of publication, to qualify for a reverse mortgage, you must be age sixty-two or older, have paid off your mortgage or have only a small balance left. The house must be your principal residence. Single-family homes are eligible; other types of housing, including multiple-unit owner-occupied dwellings and condos may be eligible. Mobile homes and co-ops are typically not eligible. Money from reverse mortgages may affect eligibility for certain public benefits programs if the money obtained is held by the borrower long enough to be considered a "liquid asset," so structuring the loan properly is important. Two federal programs are the Home Equity Conversion Mortgage (HECM), administered by the U.S. Department of Housing and Urban Development (HUD) and the Home Keeper Reverse Mortgage Loan, administered by Fannie Mae. Private programs, such as Financial Freedom, Generation Mortgage, Bank of America, and others offer their own proprietary reverse mortgage products. Call 1-800-569-4287, toll-free, to find a HUD-approved housing counseling agency. For more information on the Home Keeper for Home Purchase loan, call Fannie Mae's Consumer Resource Center at 1-800-7FANNIE or 1-800-732-6643.

PROPERTY AND REAL ESTATE TERMS TO KNOW

Depreciation: The amount your property has decreased in value due to age or wear.

Fee simple absolute: An interest in real property that is held by an individual, his or her heirs and assigns forever, without being subject to any limitations. Upon the owner's death, if no other arrangement has been made, the owner's heirs automatically inherit the property.

Incorporeal interests: Rights of a user or authority to enforce use agreements related to real property. Examples of incorporeal interests are easements and licenses.

Intangible property: See *Personal property.*

Life estate: An interest in property that is limited by the life of an individual, such as the person (the *life tenant*) to whom a property is granted as a life estate. A life tenant has the right to exclusively possess and use the property (land) and can even grant these rights to someone else up until the death of the life tenant. The life tenant's rights are also subject to the property owner's being able to enter the property to collect rent and make repairs.

Personal property: Physical items owned by a person, including furniture, clothing, jewelry, and other household furnishings not fixed to the building (also known as *tangible property*) and animals; or intellectual property (also known as *incorporeal property* or *intangible property*), such as copyrights and patents. Stocks and bonds are also considered incorporeal personal property. Personal property that has become attached to the land or to a building built on the land (for example, a bathroom fixture such as a towel rack) becomes *real property.*

Real estate: A term for land and anything that is permanently affixed to it, for example, buildings (and items attached to buildings, such as plumbing, lights, heating equipment) and fences.

Real estate agent: Someone who is licensed to represent a buyer or a seller in a real-estate transaction. Typically they are paid a commission and work for a realtor.

Real property: Land and anything that has been built on it or is growing on it. Also see *Personal property.*

Realtor: A registered trademark of the National Association of Realtors (NAR) that designates agents, brokers, and associates who are members of a real-estate firm associated with the NAR. Realtors are trained and licensed to assist clients in the purchase and/or sale of their properties.

Remainder: A property right that isn't in existence yet, but which will come into existence at a specified time in the future. For example, let's say Joe owns a piece of property. He has two siblings, Jennifer and Dan. Joe deeds or wills the property to Dan for life, and upon Dan's death, to Jennifer or to Jennifer's children if she is no longer alive when Dan dies. Jennifer's future interest in the property is a remainder and her children have a "contingent remainder."

Replacement cost: The amount it would cost to buy the same items today.

Tangible property: See *Personal property.*

RESOURCES

American Society of Appraisers
555 Herndon Parkway, Suite 125, Herndon, VA 20170
Phone: 703-478-2228; Fax: 703-742-8471
Web site: www.appraisers.org

American Moving & Storage Association
Web site: www.moving.org

Appraisal Institute® Headquarters
550 W. Van Buren Street, Suite 1000, Chicago, IL 60607
Web site: www.appraisalinstitute.org

Appraisers Association of America, Inc.
386 Park Avenue South, Suite 2000, New York, NY 10016
Phone: 212-889-5404, ext.10; Fax: 212-889-5503
Web site: www.appraisersassoc.org

American Home Inventory Protection
10513 Big Horn Dr., Fredericksburg, VA 22407
Phone: 540-273-3350
Web site: www.americanhomeip.com

Asset Recording Services, Inc.
Phone: 888-490 4277
Web site: www.assetrecordingservices.com

Board of Certification for Professional Organizers (BCPO®)
2492 Bayshore Boulevard, Suite 201, Dunedin, FL 34698
Phone 1-800-556-0484; Fax 1-727-734-9578
Web site: www.certifiedprofessionalorganizers.org

Confidential Estate Inventory
Publication available online from NAB Foundation at:
Web site: http://www.ceif.org/images/64449/US_Estate_InventoryFoundation.pdf

MoveSeniors.com™ national network of Certified Relocation & Transition Specialists (CRTS)
Assisting adults 55 and older;
Phone: 800-519-7316
Web site: www.moveseniors.com

Moving Companies
Web site: www.justmoving.org

National Association of Professional Organizers (NAPO®)
15000 Commerce Parkway, Suite C, Mount Laurel, NJ 08054
Phone: 856-380-6828; Fax: 856-439-0525
Web site: www.napo.net

National Resource Center on Supportive Housing & Home Modifications
USC Andrus Gerontology Center, Los Angeles, CA 90089-0191
Phone: 213-740-1364; Fax: 213-740-7069
Web site: www.homemods.org

Reverse Mortgage Guide
Web site: www.reversemortgageguides.org

Senior Relocation Services, National Care Planning Council
Web site: www.longtermcarelink.net/a7seniorrelocation_SRES.htm

U.S. Department of Housing and Urban Development
451 7th Street S.W., Washington, DC 20410
Phone: 202-708-1112
Web site: www.hud.gov

Chapter 4:
Health Care

MY DOCUMENTS AT-A-GLANCE

Fill in the chart below to keep track of where your critical documents will be stored and who will have access to them.

DOCUMENT	LOCATION	ACCESS/COPY GIVEN TO
Assisted living/care facility documents/home care/ nurse documents		
Health care proxy		
Health insurance card		
Health insurance documents		
Living will		
Long-term care insurance policy		
Medical records		
Medicare card		
Other		

TRACKING MEDICAL RECORDS

As you get your affairs in order, you'll want to pay particular attention to keeping track of your medical records: written or electronic records of your health history, including but not limited to descriptions of medical conditions, illnesses, diagnoses, test results, X-rays, diagnostic reports, treatments, prescriptions, medical referrals, names of attending physicians or other care providers, doctor's office visits, and hospital and testing facility visits. These records are typically prepared and maintained by a physician, hospital, or other provider of services, but you may request copies of them as well. They contain *private health information (PHI)*, which by law must be protected from viewing or retrieval by individuals to whom you have not given permission to access them.

Maintaining your own *personal health record (PHR)* allows you to monitor your health status and identify changes in physical and mental health so that you can address them before they adversely affect your lifestyle, finances, and relationships. Of course, no matter how careful anyone is to protect his or her health, chances are we'll need serious medical care at some point. Having an up-to-date medical history can communicate important information to your caregivers in the event of illness or emergency, enabling them to give you the best care possible. Finally, important decisions about health care, in the event of serious or terminal illness, and end-of-life care are best made when we aren't ill or stressed. By drafting certain kinds of documents, you can choose people to speak on your behalf should you become incapacitated. They will be entrusted with communicating your care, lifestyle, and end-of-life preferences to future caregivers and decision-makers.

In this chapter, you'll learn how to organize important information your caregivers will need, such as your medical history. We'll also discuss important documents that will allow you to communicate your treatment wishes, such as the durable power of attorney for health care, living wills, and other medical directives. Finally, this chapter will help you understand some of the options available to adults who need assistance taking care of themselves due to illness or age.

ACCURATE PERSONAL HEALTH RECORDS
CAN SAVE YOUR LIFE

Medical errors are a leading cause of injury and death; at least one report, *To Err Is Human: Building a Safer Health System* (2000) edited by the Committee on Quality of Health Care in America, Institute of Medicine, claims that more people die annually from medical errors than from motor vehicle accidents, breast cancer, or AIDS. That's why it's vital for you to keep accurate and complete records of your health status, health care providers, medications, and medical services you use and to store them in a central location. You'll want to let your loved ones know where those records are in case an emergency occurs and they need quick access to your medical history. Having all of your records in one place can help prevent medical errors by providing uniform information about your health to all of your health providers, assisting them in coordinating your care. In addition, keeping detailed records will help medical providers quickly pinpoint changes in your health status and any reasons for changes in your condition. Keeping a detailed medical record yourself helps you talk knowledgeably to your health care provider, and it can help you remember details of your visits and important medical instructions. It may help prompt you or your health care representative to ask questions if you are unsure of any aspect of your condition, including its diagnosis and the proposed treatment plan. A medical record can prevent duplicate procedures and tests and quickly get medical personnel up to speed on your health history and medical conditions in the event of an emergency. It may, in fact, save your life.

A centralized repository of your health care information can also help you manage the money that is available for treatment. It can help you track medical payments and understand how your medical benefits have been applied, what the charges for your treatment are, how much your insurance will pay, and how much you may have to pay out of your own pocket. This is important especially when we become eligible for Medicare. Medicare does not cover all health care costs, and people on Medicare typically have limited incomes. That is why some people opt for Medicare supplement insurance — to provide extra coverage for medical expenses Medicare does not pay for, like hospital deductibles. (Of course, if you have opted to purchase additional health care insurance, you'll have even more information to organize and coordinate!)

Good News and Bad about Online and Portable Electronic Records

A centralized repository for heath care records is considered so important by the treatment community that many health insurance companies, hospitals, and federal agencies are establishing online health care records for patients. For example, many health insurers will allow you to view benefits, health statements, and explanations of benefits online currently and are promising online access to comprehensive personal health records for plan participants in the near future. For example, the United States Department of Veteran's Affairs has an online portal called My Health*e*Vet (MHV) that allows veterans to access trusted health information, keep a personal health journal, view prescription information, and access benefits and resources. In the future, MHV registrants will also be able to view appointments, copay balances, and portions of their VA medical records online. (Visit www.myhealth.va.gov for more information.)

There is a downside to automated record-keeping systems, though. They may be limited to data uploaded by a single company, such as a specific health insurance plan, and that information, uploaded from claims records, may not be "vetted." That is, if a claim was inaccurately identified or processed, the information will be uploaded even though it is not correct. Also, any health care paid for outside of the insurance company may not be uploaded at all.

Another acknowledged difficulty with many of the online medical record-keeping systems offered is that access to them may be limited or take time to access. You may have some medical records stored at one location and others at another. If you are admitted to a hospital on an emergency basis, records kept elsewhere may take a while for the emergency provider to access.

What would be best, say the experts, is a single, comprehensive medical record stored in a portable device that can easily be grabbed and taken with you to whatever place you go for treatment and care. A whole new personal health record industry has sprung up to meet the demand. Products may be paper-based, Internet-based, or created using software programs on your computer. Some manufacturers, like World Medical Center (www.wmc-card.com) offer consumer "smart cards," small cards encoded with your medical history. "Thumb drives," tiny key-sized devices that can be attached to your key chain, such as VitalKey (www.vitalkey.com), are another option. To view these and dozens more that are available, go to www. myphr.com. Before deciding to purchase one of these systems, however, be sure you understand how information is kept secured, who will have access to your records, and what the hiring practices are of the company creating the record. Keep in mind that third-party management of your files may increase the risk that others — people you do not know — may be able to view your private health care information. For an overview of these issues and concerns and a list of resources that can help you understand them, visit the Electronic Privacy Information Center at www.epic.org and the Privacy Rights Clearinghouse, a nonprofit consumer advocacy organization, at ww.privacyrights.org.

The personal health record industry makes the case that having official medical records is important, since a physician may hesitate to trust a patient's own health journal. While that may be true, the fact is most doctors create treatment plans in part by interviewing the patient and taking an oral history of symptoms. Often a doctor will have to rely on a patient's recollection of past treatments or "what the other doctor told me." A health journal or a personal medical record can play a positive role here because it provides a record of our symptoms, experiences, and visits to medical professionals so we don't have to rely on remembering every little detail ourselves. It helps to put the patient more in control of his or her health care. And if we keep a detailed written history, we have something to rely on when our memory may be strained because we are feeling ill or stressed.

The technically savvy consumer can create his or her own portable medical record. Copies of official medical documents (although not X-ray film and some other diagnostic scans) can easily be scanned into a home computer and then be uploaded in a couple of clicks to a generic thumb drive or CD purchased from any office or computer supply store. A summary of current medical status and issues will give an emergency-room doctor a high-level picture, while supporting claims, medical test results, and other important medical documents (downloaded from your insurance company's online Web site and then uploaded to the drive or disk) will provide more detail.

How Do You Get Copies of Your Health Records?

Simply ask. Many people don't realize that they have the right to copies of their own medical records. In times past, the doctor, not the patient, kept the records, and a physician might even refuse to allow a patient copies of his or her own health history. That's not the case any more. The Federal Health Insurance Portability and Accountability Act (HIPAA) gives you the right to view and obtain copies of your own medical records, except in a few instances, such as psychotherapy notes. (Read more about HIPAA at the U.S. Department of Health and Human Services, www.hhs.gov, which also handles HIPAA-related complaints.) You can be charged a "reasonable" fee to cover the cost of copying the records. Your doctors' policies regarding copying your records will usually be included in a "Notice of Privacy" that they give patients to inform them of rights regarding medical records and privacy (another change that resulted from HIPAA). The doctor or medical facility will expect you to submit a written request for your records. A simple letter asking the doctor to send a copy of your complete medical record to you at your address, together with information identifying who you are (for example, your name, birth date, insurance provider, and insurance ID number), and an acknowledgment that you expect to be billed for reasonable copying fees, should suffice.

Once you have your medical records, keep them together in one place, such as a ring or other binder, for easy, "one-stop" access. Also copy them to your personal electronic PHR if you're keeping one of your own. Then, whenever you visit a care provider, be sure to ask the office for a copy of notes or results from tests while you're there. If you inform the attendant that you want a copy before you visit with the doctor, you may even be able to get a copy as you leave. Then you can add that information to your binder and/or electronic storage device when you get home.

Your Health Care Providers

Organizing medical records and creating a comprehensive personal heath record can take time. A good place to start the process is by compiling a high-level list of your care providers and their contact information, beginning with your primary care physicians and following with any specialty providers, such as a cardiac or other specialist. Next to each provider's contact information, note any ongoing medical conditions (for example, blood pressure issues, arthritis, diabetes, allergies, cancer, thyroid problems, high blood cholesterol, and so forth) as well as the treatment you're receiving. Be sure to include medications you are taking, along with the dosage. Also include any vitamins or supplements that you are taking. If something unexpected happens to you and your physician needs to be contacted for more information, this overview will at least provide some direction for those trying to manage your care.

HEALTH CARE PROVIDERS AT-A-GLANCE

PHYSICIAN NAME/ ADDRESS	MY MEDICAL CONDITION	PRESCRIPTION/TREATMENT

From the Expert

Dr. Sonya Naryshkin, on the importance of keeping personal health records

Sonya Naryshkin, M.D., F.I.A.C., F.C.A.P., a physician, nationally recognized medical quality assurance expert, patient safety consultant, and legislative advocate, says one of the best things you can do to help effectively manage your own health care is to maintain your own set of medical records.

- It's idealistic to completely rely on some other person or institution to keep your medical records for you. We no longer live in the 1950s, where one's family doctor provided continuity of care from cradle to grave. **Today, the health care system is fragmented.**

- **Often, people are being treated by multiple specialists, each addressing only one aspect of an individual's health.**

- Facilities use locum tenens — physicians who work only temporarily at any one location. There may be a string of different physicians treating a patient for a single issue.

- More facilities are using hospitalists, which are employed physicians who take care of patients while hospitalized only, and thus don't have prior personal knowledge of one's unique medical issues.

- Corporately run medical clinics can have high physician and staff turnover.

- **Even in an 'integrated' health system with computerized records, the records may not be easily or immediately accessible to the physician who is treating you.**

- All of this makes tracking a patient's health history more complicated and makes it difficult to access possibly critical medical information in a timely fashion.

- **Each time a new physician recounts your medical history, there is opportunity for errors that are then carried on to future medical records.** This has happened to me personally more than once.

- In an age where it is common for medical practices, hospitals, clinics, and medical centers to merge or get bought out by another entity, it is simply dangerous for a patient — or someone who is caring for a dependent loved one — to rely on their doctor's office for complete medical records. **If you have a medical emergency, or need to see an unfamiliar physician for an urgent problem, the few days or weeks it could take to retrieve your pertinent medical records could be fatal.** Knowledge of such things as drug allergies or sensitivities, a rare blood type, prior anesthetic complications, current medications, and active medical conditions such as diabetes could make a great difference in your care.

- **A personal health form is worth a thousand words.** If you have a form, you can just fill in the blanks, with the help of your physician if necessary. Then you know you are covered by having the essential information accessible when you need it to give to a doctor. You can photocopy your form, put it in your wallet, and even give it to a family member. If your neighbor down the street takes you to the hospital, he or she something to give to the doctor right away. This could be a lifesaving tool.

A Legal Look at Health Care

More companies are adopting consumer driven health care plans, and being able to understand your benefits can help you manage your health care spending. A number of important pieces of legislation outline the rights and responsibilities of individuals under the law with regard to health care and other employee benefits.

The **Employee Retirement Income Security Act (ERISA)** offers protection, rights to information, and an appeals process if you are enrolled in pension, health, and other benefit plans sponsored by a private-sector employer. ERISA requires certain plan administrators to make available a plan document and provide a *summary plan description/summary plan document (SPD)* to plan participants. The plan document contains important information about a health care, retirement, or other benefits plan and is usually the "last word" when it comes to deciding what your actual benefits are. The SPD also summarizes basic information about your benefits plan, including plan rules (for example, when you can participate), how benefits and services are calculated, when the benefits become vested, how to file claims, financial information (for example, what copayments you are responsible for), and how it operates, is managed, and the process whereby it can be changed or discontinued. Requests for a plan document, which is the actual document that governs the benefits plan, should be made in writing.

The **Consolidated Omnibus Budget Reconciliation Act (COBRA)** gives eligible retirees or formerly employed individuals, their spouses, and dependent children, the right to temporarily continue group health plan coverage at group rates, in certain instances.

The **Health Insurance Portability and Accountability Act (HIPAA)** provides numerous protections, including one that helps protect the privacy of *private health information (PHI)* and another prohibiting discrimination in health care coverage.

The **Patient Self-Determination Act (PSDA)** requires all health care facilities receiving Medicare or Medicaid funds to inform patients about advance directives and their right to refuse medical treatment.

The **Medicare Modernization Act (MMA)** imposes a late enrollment penalty on individuals who do not maintain creditable coverage for a period of sixty-three days or longer following their initial enrollment period for the Medicare prescription drug benefit.

The **Mental Health Parity Act** states that annual or lifetime dollar limits on mental health benefits cannot be less than those dollar limits for medical and surgical benefits offered by a group health plan.

The **Tax Equity and Fiscal Responsibility Act of 1982 (TEFRA)** defines coverage responsibilities of the Medicare program.

The **Uniform Billing Code of 1992 (UB-92)** is a federal directive that states a hospital must provide patients with itemized bills.

The **Women's Health and Cancer Rights Act** protects the right of breast cancer patients to elect breast reconstruction in connection with a mastectomy.

Additional Information to Include on Your Personal Health Record

Once you have the basic provider information listed, you can gradually add other important information to the record. Some of the things you might want to include are:

✓ Vital statistics (name, address, birth date, employer name, and contact information)

✓ Vital signs (height, weight, blood pressure)

✓ Medical and diagnostic test results

✓ Any conditions you have or have had (for example, high blood pressure, high blood cholesterol, diabetes)

✓ Any allergies you have, including to medications

✓ Details of any infections diseases (for example, chicken pox, measles, scarlet fever) that you've had

✓ Lifestyle habits (whether you smoke, drink alcohol or coffee, how often you exercise)

✓ Details of any hospitalizations or surgeries

✓ Immunization history

✓ Any family history of chronic diseases (for example, cancer, heart disease, diabetes, etc.)

It's easy to feel a bit overwhelmed when compiling health information records if you try to collect every little detail, no matter what. But keep in mind not every piece of information has the same weight when figuring out how to provide immediate treatment for someone. This is based on a typical health history form that most doctors ask new patients to fill out. If you have more questions about what is useful for your medical provider to know, you might ask your physician for a copy of his or her new patient information sheet and ask for additional guidance in setting priorities. The issue is really not to provide every detail about every doctor visit — only the important pieces of your medical history that could affect care and medical decisions made now and in the near future. It's not necessary for you to provide a decade of annual blood test results. More likely, your doctor would only be interested in seeing the results of the last few years. Would your doctor need to know that you scraped your knee when you were eight, if it didn't lead to any serious or permanent condition? Probably not. But he or she might want to know that you had the chicken pox — or have been vaccinated against it — as a child or when you first showed signs of a chronic disease, such as diabetes or high blood pressure.

CONSIDERING YOUR ADVANCE DIRECTIVE OPTIONS

Your concern about the well-being of your loved ones' is no doubt a motivating factor in getting your affairs in order. You're taking protective measures now so their welfare will be protected should you become seriously ill or incapacitated. Think about those you care about most. How would a serious, but temporary illness affect their financial status quo? Who will pay for your care and medical treatment? How will your care and treatment impact your family's time and financial resources? Take these concerns to an insurance specialist; there may be health insurance, disability, and other insurance products that can help protect your family's lifestyle, provide income, and protect your assets in the event of severe or terminal illness. By planning for unforeseen health care matters in advance, you can help yourself and your loved ones.

Advance Directives, Orders, and Other Health Care Documents

Do you want to have a say in determining what kind of medical care you'll receive if you become seriously, but temporarily, ill, incapacitated, mentally incompetent, or terminally ill? Or do you prefer to let a care provider, personal friend, family member, or state law make a decision on your behalf? How do you know whose opinion will matter most if you leave no guidance? (And even if you do?)

Conflicts often arise when a loved one becomes incapacitated, and various family members cannot agree on one method of treatment. We are fortunate to live in a country that provides us with a number of options for communicating our wishes to our caregivers when we are seriously ill or in the event we become unable to make decisions for ourselves. Once we have decided how we want to be treated in the event of extreme illness or if we become incapable of managing our own health care, we need to take certain steps to ensure that our wishes will be followed. The majority of documents in the section below are "advance directives"— documents designed to help us communicate our desires clearly and effectively, and with legal backing. These documents provide essential directives or authorization to those who will be managing our health care decisions. Samples of these documents can be obtained through the organizations listed at the end of this chapter. State laws vary regarding documents designed to direct our health care when we become incapacitated, so be sure to check with your local hospital, state medical or nursing association, or state bar association to find out more about what regulations apply in your state.

"My insurance company automatically posts a personal health record online for each plan participant. Some basic information can be input by the employee, but most of it is automatically uploaded from claims documents. Out of curiosity, I decided to review mine, and was surprised and somewhat dismayed to learn that my annual OB-GYN exam was processed as a "general psychiatric exam" under the plan's mental health benefits, and several visits to my GP for a cold were also processed as mental health visits. I called the company to address this matter, which I suspected was probably the result of a coding error from an overworked coder, but the online health record provider customer service representative said she could not help me correct the information. After much questioning, I learned there was a box I could check to deny access to my personal health record to others, which I checked. I was surprised to learn that I had to ask for the records to be restricted; I would have thought the opposite — that they would be restricted unless I indicated otherwise. Now I've got to review the rest of the record and spend my time following up on inaccuracies with letters to the hospitals and physicians who coded the claims incorrectly. "—*Marcella, age 52*

An *advance directive* is a document prepared by an individual in advance of becoming incapacitated that provides guidance in the event that he or she becomes unable to make decisions and takes effect when the individual becomes incompetent. A medical advance directive designates a surrogate to make decisions about your health care or provides direction for your health care and documents your treatment preferences. By law, medical facilities that receive Medicare or Medicaid funding, such as hospitals and nursing homes, must provide information about advance care directives in writing to all patients upon admission. Common issues addressed by advance medical directives include treatments that may help to prolong life artificially, such as tube or intravenous feeding, blood transfusions, the use of cardiopulmonary resuscitation (CPR) after cardiac arrest, maintenance on a respirator, and certain diagnostic tests, such as blood cultures.

Before signing an advance medical directive, it is wise to get input from a physician, who can help you understand what medical language and terms mean from the patient's perspective and how these documents may be interpreted in a hospital or medical setting. Keep in mind that advance care directives can only deal with current medical practices and may become outdated as new treatments or types of care become available for situations considered terminal today. Be sure to review these documents periodically and share any decisions you make with your loved ones and caregivers.

An advance directive may take the form of a single document drafted by an attorney that provides for an integrated approach to managing health care decisions. In the opinion of some attorneys, a single, comprehensive advance directive is a better way to communicate what your wishes are to the person who will be making medical decisions on your behalf. Many physicians also believe it is best to address these concerns as part of a comprehensive treatment plan and suggest that any advance directive documents include language requiring input from a physician at all points of decision-making. Nevertheless, like many people, you may decide a specific type of directive or order by itself better addresses your concerns. For example, in the case of an accident or emergency, emergency medical personnel or paramedics may not have the time nor legal training to read and interpret a lengthy, complex document. Emergency medical personnel are focused on saving the life of the patient and will do so when they are in doubt about a patient's wishes, such as in the absence of a clear and qualified order, such as a signed do-not-resuscitate (DNR) order. Common types of advance directives and related orders are:

A *do-not-hospitalize (DNH)* order prohibits inpatient hospitalization. People sometimes sign a DNH order because they don't want to be removed from comfortable surroundings and their current care providers and taken to a hospital where they may receive expensive and uncomfortable medical interventions for situations where there is little or no hope of recovery. On the other hand, if one has signed a blanket order prohibiting removal to a hospital, then treatments that can be delivered only at a hospital may not be available to the patient. Some experts feel that requiring a physician consultation before transfer to a hospital may protect the patient's wishes and allow the avenue for treatment at a hospital to stay open should an instance arise where it can benefit the patient and support his or her goals for treatment and care. DNH orders are often drafted by physicians.

A *do-not-intubate (DNI)* order is a directive not to intubate, that is, to insert a tube into a patient's windpipe, nose, or mouth. Intubation is typically used to administer artificial nutrition, anesthetics, or oxygen, for drainage or to maintain an open air passage.

A *do-not-resuscitate (DNR)* order is a directive not to restore functionality of the heart or lungs if you suffer cardiac or respiratory arrest. Typical resuscitation methods include chest compressions (CPR), the administration of drugs or electric shock (defibrillation) to stimulate the heart, and assisted ventilation. This document can be used by an individual to direct medical personnel in the event that the individual becomes terminally ill or has a life-threatening injury and does not want to receive life-prolonging emergency medical treatment or be put on artificial life support. An "in-hospital" DNR is an order that you ask your physician to add to your medical record when you are in the hospital. Another kind of DNR is a "pre-hospital" DNR, which is a document you may keep in your wallet or with you at home (or wherever you're living), or an order engraved on a medallion worn around your neck or on a bracelet, such as a "MedicAlert" medallion bracelet, that communicates your wishes to emergency medical technicians (EMTs) called in the event of an emergency. (The "MedicAlert" medallion bracelet also can be used to provide your critical medical information or personal health record to emergency personnel; for general information about MedicAlert, visit online at www.medicalert.org. For more information about DNR and advance directives repository services, contact MedicAlert Foundation at 888-633-4298.) A DNR does not prevent the administration of all types of emergency care; treatment for pain, bleeding, and other medical conditions is typically provided. State laws and local policies, forms, and procedures also vary; contact your local emergency medical services (EMS) agency for information about them.

Five Wishes is a document written in easy-to-understand language that will help you document which person you want to make health care decisions for you when you can't make them, the kind of medical treatment you want or don't want, how you'd like to be treated, and more. As of this printing, the group Aging With Dignity, which provides *Five Wishes*, states on its Web site that the document is legally valid in forty states, although some of those states may place certain restrictions on its use or have additional requirements. In states where *Five Wishes* is not valid, the organization notes that you can contact the state for a form that addresses some of the points covered in *Five Wishes* and then attach the more detailed *Five Wishes* document to the form to provide additional information and support. For more information, or to purchase a copy for a nominal fee, contact Aging With Dignity. The actual document may be viewed at: http://www.agingwithdignity.org/5wishes.html.

A *living will* (not to be confused with a will) explains how you want to be treated if you are unable to direct your own medical care. It authorizes your health care provider, or an individual that you have designated to speak for you under a separate document, such as a durable medical power of attorney or a health care proxy, to discontinue medical treatments in certain circumstances should you become unable to speak on your own behalf. For example, an individual might direct her doctor to discontinue use of a respirator in the event that she becomes severely brain damaged or is in a coma for a prolonged period of time, has an incurable or irreversible injury, disease, illness or condition, or enters a persistent vegetative state. Other life-prolonging procedures that are typically addressed in a living will are artificial or "tube" feeding, the use of medications, medical testing, blood transfusions, cardiopulmonary resuscitation (CPR), dialysis, and surgery. Another name for this type of a document is a *Health Care Declaration or Directive to Physicians*, which communicates to your health care provider what medical procedures you want performed and what type of care you wish to be given in the event that you are unable to speak on your own behalf.

• Few people think of them as such, but an *organ donation card* is also a type of advance directive. This card, usually filled out when renewing a driver's license (and sometimes incorporated in the information on one) is typically carried in a wallet. It provides instructions for the donation of your eyes and other organs in the event of a fatal accident. In addition to your state Department of Motor Vehicles, hospitals and other medical centers can provide you with information about becoming an organ donor. Keep a copy of the donor card with your other advance directives.

• *POST (Physician Orders for Scope of Treatment)* is a standardized form that you can use to express your medical treatment preferences before you need medical treatment. It may include a DNR instruction and may provide a wristband identifying this instruction to be worn by the patient. A physician may supply and help you complete the form.

Appointing Someone to Manage Your Health Care on Your Behalf

In addition to stating your wishes in one of the above documents, you can appoint someone to represent you and ensure your wishes are carried out should you become incapacitated.

As noted in Chapter 2, a *durable power of attorney* for health care is a legal document, usually drafted with the help of an attorney, which allows you to designate an individual to make decisions about your medical treatment in the event that you are unable to. The individual you designate in a durable medical power of attorney will be able to make decisions about your medical treatment, even if you have not provided them with any instructions, which is one reason you should be sure to choose a person you can trust who understands your wishes. Another term for a *durable power of attorney for health care* that authorizes someone to make health care decisions for you when you are unable to do so is *health care power of attorney*. You might also hear the terms *health care proxy, agent, representative,* or *surrogate* used to refer to a person authorized to make health care and medical treatment decisions on your behalf. The individual you appoint will be able to make decisions about your medical treatment, even if you have not provided him or her with any instructions, which is one reason you should be sure to choose a person you can trust to understand your wishes. You should feel comfortable giving that person access to your medical and financial records, and feel that he or she has the confidence and intelligence to ask informed questions of medical personnel. If you have provided instructions (for example, in a living will), the person designated as your health care proxy will be empowered to interpret the instructions you've left. A health care proxy form can usually be obtained at a hospital or medical center and is usually filled out without a lawyer's help.

Understanding Treatment Options

Making informed decisions about serious illness or end-of-life care is not a simple matter, because it does require some understanding of various types of illness and treatment options. In other words, you'll need to be an informed health care consumer to figure out whether the treatment options you're considering asking for at end-of-life can potentially benefit you. To become more informed, you may want to do some additional research to educate yourself about clinical definitions of what constitutes incapacity and terminal illness. You'll also need to understand something about treatment options and so-called "heroic" measures that may prolong life in the event of a terminal medical condition, including cardiopulmonary resuscitation (CPR), intubation for feeding, artificial or mechanical respiration, organ transplants, antibiotics, defibrillation, dialysis, blood transfusions, surgery, and other life-support systems.

Start by asking yourself what the term "quality of life" means to you, because decisions may need to be made about your treatment when your quality of life is impacted; for example, if you experience reduced mobility or become incapacitated or terminally ill. Discuss with a health care provider what the benefits of commonly available life-sustaining treatments are as well as their drawbacks. Do you want any available treatment, regardless of cost, even if your doctor or care provider believes your prognosis is poor? Or will you refuse treatments or medical interventions that may cause other parts of your body not to function as well as they might otherwise? Before crafting a medical directive or appointing a health care proxy, you should also give some thought to your spiritual values. Do you have any religious beliefs that could affect your care choices or end-of-life options? Under what circumstances, if any, would you want life-sustaining treatments to be withdrawn?

Discussing options with a caring physician, member of the clergy, or friend or relative whose opinions you respect, can help. There are also many non-profit organizations that have posted information about advance directives and end-of-life choices — albeit from sometimes conflicting points of view — on the Web. Other possible sources of help are social agencies, community or non-profit organizations, federal, state, or local agencies, and legal advisors or groups.

Limits of Advance Directives

Sometimes the decisions that must be made when caring for an individual, especially one who may be near end-of-life, are complex and cannot be known in advance, so the information in the medical directive may not necessarily apply to a specific situation. The facility at which you are receiving care may also have policies that can affect an interpretation of your document or any change to it. Therefore, you may also want to ask what the process is if you find yourself in a care facility and your health care representative wishes to question your medical treatment or prefers to try another approach. If a conflict arises, will there be access to mediation? What steps should be taken if an unforeseen conflict arises between your health care representative and your care providers, the clinical team that's providing treatment, a medical facility, social agency or social worker, governmental body, or your family and friends? Who will the final decision-maker be? How will the care facility's institutional guidelines impact care or the directive that's been put in place?

Keep in mind that having an advance directive, while helpful, cannot always guarantee a particular outcome. If the documents have not been included in your patient record, if your doctor or health care proxy is unaware of the document, if it isn't properly worded, or it's determined you were incompetent while crafting it, it may not impact your health care at all. Medical facilities may also have requirements for implementing advance directives, such as requiring two independent medical practitioners to confirm that the patient is not likely to regain capacity in the near future. That's why it's important to contact an attorney, preferably one with a background in elder care, or your state department of aging, to ask about which of these documents are accepted by state law, and to find out any steps you need to take to make them accepted as legal documents. For example, your state may require a document to be notarized and signed in the presence of one or more witnesses or it may require your doctor's signature.

Be sure to provide copies of your documents to those who need them — for example, request a directive to be placed in your medical record. You may also wish to have it recorded on an ID tag so you can wear it (for example, a "do-not-resucitate" tag) and have it available in case of an emergency. You may want to keep a copy in your wallet. If you have a health care proxy or representative, you'll need to give them copies. You, or your representative, should attach a copy to your medical records as well as notify your physician and any hospital or medical facility about the existence of these documents upon admission. Either you, or your health care representative, should be sure that it's recorded in your care plan and wherever the medical staff keeps patient notes.

In an emergency, you may be taken to a hospital or facility or be treated by an emergency medical team that won't be aware of your advance directive unless you or someone else tells them. That's why it's important to talk with family, friends, and care providers about your preferences and to copy it onto a card or metal medallion that you carry with you.

Review the document on a regular basis. Consult your doctor to be sure it reflects "best practices" and current treatment options and talk to an attorney about what can be done to ensure it's used — and, incidentally, what steps you need to take if you change your mind in the future.

Also be sure you understand the process of canceling or amending a directive if you change your mind, including who you'll need to notify or send a revised copy to. You should plan to review these documents periodically as you grow older, when your health changes or you become ill, if you go through a life-changing circumstance, such as a divorce or marriage, if you give birth to a child (but note that many states won't consider these documents valid if signed when pregnant), or if a spouse, parent, or child dies.

"Coming down with a serious illness made me realize how important it was to have a legal document outlining my preferences for care if I became incapacitated or was dying. I was especially worried about having someone else's religious beliefs imposed on me. I just didn't want to be kept alive indefinitely if I became unconscious, fed through tubes, or anything like that. I'd heard about the *Five Wishes* document. Reading it gave me the courage to consult an attorney. After meeting with him, I opted for a document that he drew up instead. It was easy to do — much easier than I had expected. All I had to do was answer questions about my preferences. Once I was asked the questions, I found them easy to answer. I am so relieved."

— Essie, age 70

My Health Insurance At-A-Glance

Health Insurance Company Name: _____

Phone #:_____

Kind of Plan:_____

Subscriber ID:_____ Policy #:_____

Deductible: $_____

Health Insurance Company Name: _____

Phone #:_____

Kind of Plan:___ _____ _____

Subscriber ID:_____ Policy #:_____

Deductible: $_____

Benefits Plan Documents

To properly process health claims, and to estimate health care expenses, it's important to have a complete understanding of your health benefits plan(s). Summary plan documents and fees schedules provide a quick, high-level overview of your benefits, but more detailed information will most likely be needed if an illness is serious or complex. Your spouse, family member, or health care proxy will need to be able to access your health care plan information, including policy information, benefits manager contact information, and plan document, which describes your benefits in detail, as well as documents that describe any claims that may have been processed against your benefits, health statements summarizing your recent treatments, relevant correspondence you may have had with benefits managers, and outstanding bills and other benefits-related financial documents.

FINDING SOCIAL, EMOTIONAL, OR SPIRITUAL SUPPORT

The purpose of this section is to help you take control of end-of-life decisions. In many non-emergency situations, you have more power than you think about the choices that need to be made, including how you are treated — and where. There are steps you can take to ensure that your last days can be spent at home or in another place of your choice. Hospice care, covered under Part A of Medicare, is one option. Hospice care is designed to keep those who are dying physically comfortable and emotionally supported and to provide support to their families. Often this is a multidisciplinary approach within a special institutional setting or a facility dedicated to providing comfort to people in their final days, but nurses or other caregivers at the person's home can also provide it. Medicare equipment and personnel are brought to your house and care provided for you in your final hours, so you can be in a familiar environment, surrounded by loved ones.

You also can ask for specific kinds of treatments that will help make your ending more comfortable, such as certain kinds of pain medication. Palliative care services are designed to reduce or relieve symptoms associated with terminal illness, or reduce its progress, and to promote quality of life during the time that remains. For example, if someone has a tumor that cannot be surgically removed, the focus of treatment would be reducing its growth rate and managing pain.

At all times you have the right to informed consent, which means you should only make a decision about medical treatment or a procedure after being provided with relevant and appropriate information, including but not limited to information about the diagnosis, purpose of treatment, risks and consequences and other care options. In case you are unable to speak for yourself or are mentally incapacitated and therefore are unable to give informed consent, you can include directions for palliative care in your durable medical power of attorney or other directive to a health care proxy. Some of the specific issues to address are under what circumstances you would want to receive pain medication, whether it's OK for you to be given medication to remain comfortable, even if it may make you sleepy or possibly hasten death (or, conversely, whether, due to religious beliefs, you prefer to receive no pain medication at all or to receive it only if it does not in any way impact your ability to stay alive). You or your designated health care representative also have the right to refuse extraordinary measures intended to prolong life after a physician has determined that you are terminally ill.

Decisions for end-of-life care extend beyond the purely medical. For example, perhaps you'd like someone to be by your side at all times, or to be held. You might also like to have ongoing emotional support from a clergy person, grief counselor, psychologist, spiritual advisor, social worker, family, friend or other caregiver, or to arrange such support for your loved ones. Perhaps you'd like to be groomed, listen to music, watch videos, read a special book, have someone say prayers, or have a special picture or beautiful floral arrangement next to your bedside during your final hours.

Capturing Your Final Wishes

Once you've decided on how you'd like to be treated if you become incapacitated or when you become ill or near end-of-life, it's important to get your thoughts down on paper. Meet with your professional advisors — your attorney, financial advisor, clergy person, physician, and others familiar with elder care and end-of-life issues — and draft the legal documents that will protect you and your family during troubled times ahead. Set aside some time to capture any issues, desires, wishes, or concerns about medical care and treatment in a letter to your loved ones. The more specific you are, the easier it will before others to make critical decisions about your care. You can attach this letter to the important documents drafted by your attorney, such as your living will or advance medical directive and instruct your attorney to keep it in a safe place along with your will and any other legal documents. Be sure to let your family and health care representative know where the original documents are located, and be sure to provide them with copies. If you can, schedule a review with your loved ones and your proxy so you can answer any questions and address any fears or concerns they may have. You can leave your loved ones with no greater gift than the knowledge that your care and situation in your final days and hours, given the circumstances, was just as you wished.

RESOURCES

Health Care

American Association for Geriatric Psychology (AAGP)/Geriatric Mental Health Foundation
7910 Woodmont Ave., Suite 1050, Bethesda, MD 20814-3004
Phone: 301-654-7850; Fax: 301-654-4137
Web sites: www.aagpgpa.org; www.GMHFonline.org

Centers for Medicare and Medicaid Services
7500 Security Boulevard, Baltimore, MD 21244
Phone: 877-267-2323
Web sites: www.cms.hhs.gov; www.medicare.com

Medicare Rights Center (MRC)
1460 Broadway, 17th Floor, New York, NY 10036
Phone: 212-869-3850; Fax: 212-869-3532
Web site: www.medicarerights.org

National Association of Area Agencies on Aging (N4A)
1730 Rhode Island Ave. NW, Suite 1200,
Washington, D.C. 20036
Phone: 800-677-1116; 202-872-0888; Fax: 202-872-0057
Web site: www.n4a.org

Assisted Living, Dying, Terminal Illness, Palliative Care and Hospice

Americans for Better Care of the Dying
1700 Diagonal Road, Suite 635, Alexandria, VA 22314;
Phone: 703-647-8505; Fax: 703-837-1233
Web site: www.abcd-caring.org

Caring Connections, National Hospice Foundation (NHF)
1700 Diagonal Road, Suite 625, Alexandria, VA 22314
Phone: 800-658-8898; 703-837-1500; Fax: 703-837-1233;
HelpLine: 800-658-8898; Spanish HelpLine: 877-658-8896
Web sites: www.caringinfo.org; www.hospiceinfo.org;

Compassion & Choices
P.O. Box 101810, Denver, CO 80250-1810
Phone: 800-247-7421, 303-639-1224
Web site: www.compassionandchoices.org

Long-Term, Nursing, Nursing Homes & End-of-Life Care American Association of Homes and Services for the Aging (AAHSA®)
2519 Connecticut Avenue NW, Washington D.C. 20008-1520
Phone: 202-783-2242
Web site: www.aahsa.org

Assisted Living Federation of America (ALFA)
1650 King St., Suite 602, Alexandria, VA 22314
Phone: 703-894-1805; Fax: 703-894-1831
Web site: www.alfa.org

Elder Care Online™, Prism Innovations, Inc.
50 Amuxen Court, Islip, N.Y. 11751
Web site: www.ec-online.net

National Association for Home Care (NAHC)
228 7th Street, SE Washington, D.C. 20003
Phone: 202-547-7424; Fax: 202-547-3540
Web site: www.nahc.org

National Center for Assisted Living (NCAL®)
1201 L Street, NW Washington, D.C. 20005
Phone: 202-824-4444
Web site: www.ncal.org

National Citizen's Coalition for Nursing Home Reform (NCCNHR)
1828 L Street, NW, Suite 801, Washington, D.C. 20036-2211
Phone: 202-332-2276; Fax: 202-332-2949
Web site: www.nccnhr.org

National Clearinghouse for Long-Term Care Resources
U.S. Department of Health and Human resources web page,
Web site: www.aoa.gov/ownyourfuture

National Long-Term Care Ombudsman Resource Center (NLTCORC)
ORC Office 1828 L Street, NW, Suite 801,
Washington, D.C. 20036
Phone: 202-332-2275; Fax: 202-332-2949
Web site: www.ltcombudsman.org

Personal Health Records Storage

MedicAlert® Foundation
2323 Colorado Avenue, Turlock, CA 95382
Phone: 888-633-4298; 209-668-3333; Fax: 209-669-2450
Web site: www.medicalert.org

myPHR.com
A Web site of the American Health Information Management Association (AHIMA), a national non-profit professional association dedicated to the effective management of personal health information, provides lists of Internet-, paper- and software-based health record suppliers; www.myphr.com. Two it lists are: Vital Key; 2233 North Michigan Ave., 21st Floor, Chicago, IL 60601-5800; Phone: 312-233-1090; Fax: 312-233-1090 and World Medical Card, www.wmc-card.com.

NOTES

Chapter 5:
Minor Children, Dependent Family Members, and Pets

MY DOCUMENTS AT-A-GLANCE

Fill in the chart below to keep track of where your critical documents will be stored and who will have access to them.

DOCUMENT	LOCATION	ACCESS/COPY GIVEN TO
Adoption, birth, marriage, death, custody, separation, divorce papers		
Child identity records		
Citizenship papers, passports, military records		
Driver's license		
Letter of intent		
School records		

THE LETTER OF INTENT

Imagine what would happen if you were to pass away suddenly, and the person assigned to care for your children knew very little about them. Lack of knowledge about your child's preferences, personality, and daily routines can make children feel uncared for and can frustrate caregivers. The same is true if you are the guardian or primary caregiver for a dependent adult. If Uncle Johnny is afraid of birds, and a caregiver unsuspecting takes him for a walk in a city park, what was planned as a treat could result in something quite different.

Even simple tasks of parenting, such as enrolling your child in school, picking her up from school, or taking him to a doctor could be difficult. Without a birth certificate or other ID, enrolling in school is problematic. Today, no safety-minded program should allow someone to take your child from the premises without written authorization from you. And your child or adult dependent will be best cared for by a doctor who is familiar with his or her health history and has up-to-date medical records on file. Preparing to transfer the care of your child to someone else in the event that you become incapacitated is one of the most important responsibilities of parenting.

One of the easiest ways to assist potential caregivers and ensure they are equipped to address the daily lifestyle needs of your children and any adult dependents in your care is to prepare a *letter of intent*. This document is really a practical guide to all things that relate to your dependent. In the case of a child, it's the letter that you write, providing insight into his or her nature. The letter should include your child's personal history, your dreams for his or her future, and possible alternatives for your child's care. It should include basic information about the dependent, including a schedule, daily routines, and habits; personal lifestyle preferences and choices; and your wishes regarding your child's future, for example, whether you'd like him or her to be raised in a particular religion or be educated a certain way. The letter of intent is not a legal document, but it can help educate your attorney and financial planner so they can advise you on legal and financial matters relating to your dependents. In the event that something happens to you, it provides insight to those tasked with carrying out your wishes — courts, lawyers, and trustees

— and, more practically, gives your child's guardians and caregivers the information necessary to maintain the lifestyle and level of care to which your dependent is accustomed. You should keep the original letter, together with any supporting documents, including a recent photo of your child, in a safe place, such as with your will in your attorney's office and with anyone you've designated as trustee or guardian. Plan to update both the document and the photo as the years go by.

Writing the Letter of Intent

You'll use your own judgment when writing your letter of intent. No doubt it also will reflect your own personality and approach to life issues. If you aren't a writer, it may just be an economical list of some points you'd like to make, with supporting documents attached. You may decide to use the letter only to fill in the little details not already covered in a will or trust agreement (although you should at least tell the person reading the letter that those items exist and where they are to be found). On the other hand, if you are a parent who enjoys waxing poetic about your child, your letter is likely to be longer and more detailed. Whatever your style, you'll want to consider including some coverage of the topics detailed in this section in your letter.

You can begin your letter with a standard salutation, such as "To Whom It May Concern" (your lawyer can direct this letter to the child's guardian upon your

"My Aunt Katherine has a developmental disability, but she lives alone in her own apartment. I made sure it was appropriate for her physical needs, close to public transportation, and the grocery store, and there is a friendly neighbor who has my number in case something comes up. I visit Aunt Katherine regularly and take her to the beautician to get her hair and nails done, especially when there's a family function that she will be going to. She looks forward to this little ritual, and her happiness at visiting the beauty parlor is something I wouldn't want to miss — nor would I want her to miss it if something happened to me and someone else took over her care."

—*Mary Beth, age 53*

demise). The salutation can be followed by a paragraph introducing your dependent. Think of it as a short biography of your child. In addition to the dependent's legal birth name, you'll want to include whether he or she has a nickname, as well as a basic description of your child, including his or her height, weight, eye and hair color, and any other distinguishing marks. But don't stop there: also talk about your child's personality, sense of humor, and sense of self, and any gifts he or she has been blessed with.

Next, tell the reader basic information about your dependent's lifestyle, such as where and with whom he or she lives (if not with you). Detail your child's school, grade and classes, and any clubs or activities he or she is involved in. If this information is available in separate documents, such as a school schedule and directory, you may not need to go into great detail, but be sure to have the schedule and other supporting documents on hand, so that when your letter is complete, they can be attached to it and filed with the actual letter.

Include information that's likely to be the case for the foreseeable future — for example, if your child goes to camp or vacations with a certain relative, or worships in a certain religion, include that information here. If your child enjoys certain activities — like playing a certain video game, hiking outdoors, making crafts, or collecting coins — make a note of it. What are your child's favorite things or routines? Does he or she have any pets or special toys? What foods does he or she like and dislike? Also list your child's favorite books, movies, TV shows, colors and favorite items of clothing. Discuss the objects, places, or activities that could help to comfort your child during a time of need or stress. Is there a normal routine that's followed on a daily basis? The idea is to help potential caregivers understand what constitutes a normal life for your child. You'll want to provide specific information as well for an adult dependent.

Next you'll want to say something about people who are meaningful in your dependent's life. For example, does your daughter spend time after school at her grandmother's house or with another care provider? Does she have a best friend? Who is she, and what do they enjoy doing together? Who else does she hang out with?

A high-level overview of financial matters concerning your dependent can be tackled next. For example, perhaps your disabled adult has a trust fund, or you've already opened savings or investment accounts for your child. You can list the name and type of account or instrument, where it's located, who manages it (for example, a corporate trust broker, investment advisor, etc.) and their contact information, who has access to it, a description of it, and where the papers (statements, instruments of trust, etc.) are located (presumably with your other financial or legal documents or attached to the letter).

Once you've painted the picture of your dependent's present, you can move on to the future, to discuss your wishes, dreams, and aspirations for the dependent — and his or her own wishes, dreams, and aspirations as well. Some questions you might like to answer are:

- If something were to happen to me, who would be my preferred choice for guardian for the child or dependent now in my care? (List these in order of preference.)

- If something were to happen to me, who would be my preferred choice for trustee to manage finances/funds for my child/dependent now in my care?

- If something were to happen to me, where would I prefer the child or dependent now in my care to live, if not with the guardian (for example, to reside at a boarding school instead).

With these basics out of the way, it's time to think about the next section of the letter of intent — to provide information that would be helpful in fostering your dependent's personal growth in the future. Think of this as your personal guide to parenting your child in the years ahead. For example, you might begin by describing his or her level of social expertise and go on to discuss what social skills could be developed, what issues may need to be addressed, and how to address them. What motivates him or her? What methods of discipline have been effective in the past? What is the best way to communicate with your child?

Next on the agenda might be your wishes for your child's education. Questions to answer here include:

- If something were to happen to me, what options do I recommend for my child/dependent's education or vocational training?

- Does my child/dependent have the interest and ability to enroll in college or graduate school or another specialty school (for example, one that specializes in art or cooking)?

- Does she or he demonstrate any talent or skill that I'd like to see developed (for example, playing an instrument, learning a language)?

- Have I set aside any money for this in a taxed-advantaged account or in a will or other financial instrument?

Work and career come next:

- What employment possibilities might he or she explore? What career paths might be good choices?

Spirituality and ethics may be the most important point of all. In drafting this section of your letter, ask yourself:

- Do I prefer that my dependent receives some kind of training related to spiritual matters, such as being raised in a certain religion or studying a certain kind of philosophy?

- What would I like him or her to know about my personal beliefs and ethics?

- Is there any advice or perspective I would like to share regarding how to make the most of life's opportunities?

Periodically, you'll want to update the letter of intent as the need arises and as circumstances change.

Documents to Keep with the Letter of Intent

Attach to your letter of intent any supporting documents that provide relevant details as well as important information that relates to your dependent, for example:

- Paperwork that legally establishes your dependent's identity, such as a birth certificate and Social Security card or other identity papers

- Emergency contact information, in case you can't be reached

- A record of any bank accounts or other financial instruments being held in your dependent's name, together with their locations, and, if the dependent is an adult, a record of his or her income, expenses, assets, and liabilities

- Medical records and any physicians who have provided your dependent care

- School records

- The names and addresses of any people who are important to your dependent or who participate in his or her care (don't forget to note why they are important)

SPECIAL NEEDS ASSESSMENT

If one or more of your dependents is disabled, a needs or skills assessment is also useful. If the disability is severe and the individual is under care, you may already have a professionally completed needs assessment. If not, you may want to contact one of the organizations listed in the Resources section at the end of this chapter. However, if the dependent is very young, or very old, or the disability is slight, and you don't have a professionally completed one, here are some things you might want to consider providing information about.

A critical part of budgeting and financial planning for households with special needs children or disabled adults is assessing how much help is needed for the activities of daily living and whether he or she will be able to support him- or herself. While a company seeking to employ someone may be barred from asking certain questions, as a concerned parent or caregiver, honestly assessing your special needs child or dependent adult's physical limitations, level of cognitive development, appearance, and social skills can help you, and the caregivers you have selected, to match your child to available skill- development programs, educational and training programs, and employment opportunities. By providing details about things like the dependent's ability to dress or bathe, you can help caregivers plan the amount of assistance needed for the ordinary activities of daily life.

You'll also want to address questions about certain cognitive skills (for example, counting, reading) and communications skills (speech) that are typically needed to perform simple work-related tasks and may help your child to transition to a job in the workforce. For example, a developmentally disabled person who takes pride in his appearance and is very polite may be a prime candidate for a customer service job, such as helping a veterinarian's receptionist. An adult who is physically disabled may have superior reasoning and verbal skills; with special accommodations and equipment she may be able to hold down a full-time office job.

We've covered just some of the areas you'll want to explore with a qualified advisor. If your loved one is a child, you won't be as certain of his or her capabilities and potential for growth, and will want to obtain a more in-depth assessment from a professional who is experienced in helping to plan realistically for the future of a special needs child and can help you explain those plans in your letter of intent. You'll want to discuss future plans for your adult dependent as well.

"My wife was hospitalized for several months. Caring for her and dealing with her medical care, insurance, and work issues took a lot of time. Thankfully, my family and friends offered to help out. Being able to provide them with a schedule and information about things like my kids' mealtimes and food preferences made all of the difference. I truly got the help I needed, my kids weathered the storm, and, when my wife returned home, our day-to-day routines were intact."

—*Rich, age 49*

—From the Expert—

Daniel Marson, J.D., Ph.D., on the care of older adult dependents

Good health isn't something we usually associate with the ability to keep our documents organized or managing our financial affairs, but according to at least one researcher, the connection should not be overlooked. Daniel Marson, J.D., Ph.D., professor of neurology and director of the Alzheimer's Disease Research Center at the University of Alabama at Birmingham, has conducted studies that indicate that the ability to perform basic financial tasks, such as organizing documents and paying bills, can reveal something about our cognitive health. Cognitive decline, he says, often reveals itself in the inability to perform these basic financial tasks.

- Marson and his team of researchers recently published a study that found that people who are in the early stages of Alzheimer's disease show rapid decline over one year in their ability to manage their financial affairs. **The study suggests that people experiencing mild symptoms of the disease, such as forgetfulness when paying bills or difficulty with basic money matters, should act immediately to put their affairs in order while they can still make decisions.** Such steps include appointing someone to manage their affairs for them through a durable power of attorney.

- But these findings don't just apply to seniors or those who are already showing signs of cognitive impairment; the connection between cognitive health and financial well-being should put us all on notice to take better care of ourselves, no matter what our age.

- **"Your vascular and cardiac health have a lot to do with your brain health,"** says Marson. "People who develop diabetes, high blood pressure, and heart disease are at risk of developing vascular changes in the brain that can lead to cognitive impairment and, consequently, impaired abilities to handle financial matters." Conversely, he notes, "Living a heart-healthy lifestyle in your middle years helps maintain cognitive health and financial capacity in later years."

- **In addition to recommending that people keep their blood pressure, cholesterol, and weight within healthy bounds, he also recommends cognitively stimulating activities such as taking up a musical instrument, playing bridge, dancing, and engaging in social activities.** These are all ways to preserve cognitive function in later life.

- And Marson advises those who have aging family members to keep a caring and watchful eye on the health and behavior of their elders. Cognitive impairment leaves them open either to being financially exploited or to making financial mistakes, he says.

- **"It's important for family members to be mindful of their older loved ones' mental abilities and to keep track of them and their health.** I do a fair number of forensic cases, and what I see a lot of is the family staying at a distance because it doesn't want to be overly solicitous or overbearing. Then, before they know it, the loved one makes a significant error — sells property at a fraction of its value — or gets scammed.

- **"In some cases, a neighbor develops an unhealthy interest in an older person's well-being, brainwashing the person into thinking the family doesn't care about him or her anymore, and the next thing you know, there's a new will with that person named as the estate's beneficiary.** It happens more often than you think. Once the will is changed, the burden of proof to invalidate the will is on the family. It's so expensive to litigate, many times families end up settling a case that they should not be involved with in the first place."

- **Marson advises family members to be sensitive to changes in an older person's prior lifelong financial abilities, values, and behaviors.** "Warning signs, in addition to math mistakes, include disorganization (for example, an inability to keep track of bills and documents or to prepare taxes; memory lapses (forgetting to pay bills or paying them twice); general confusion about financial or estate-planning concepts (for example, the inability to understand what a loan is, despite repeated explanations); an inability to look at a financial issue from different vantage points; and an unhealthy interest in get-rich-quick schemes or sweepstakes."

- What can you do if you notice any of these signs of possible cognitive and financial impairment? "Ask informed questions. Start with 'I'm concerned,' not an ultimatum," says Marson. **"Once you've noticed something is off, get a medical evaluation to identify the problem and get a treatment plan in place. Take immediate steps to secure their financial affairs.** Work with an attorney and an accountant to secure their estate so that they will not be at financial risk."

- "I've seen so many horror stories — frank exploitation of the aged, the resources of people in late life plundered by others, in some cases, even taken by those who are caring for them. **With the tidal wave of aging now facing us, the frank exploitation of older individuals will probably become worse. It's something we all need to be aware of and to take steps to guard against."**

Legal Look: The Special Needs Trust

When drafting a will or preparing an estate plan, it's important to carefully review available state and federal benefits to determine what assistance your disabled child may be eligible for now and in the future. Support may include benefits that are paid regardless of financial need (for example, Social Security disability insurance pays benefits to your family member if you are "insured," meaning that you worked long enough and paid Social Security taxes, regardless of financial need) or benefits based on financial need, such as Supplemental Security Income (visit the Social Security Web site at http://www.socialsecurity.gov/disability/disability_starter_kits.htm for a "Disability Starter" kit). Your state laws also need to be taken into account.

If your child isn't receiving or won't be eligible for government assistance based on financial need, and he or she does not have a cognitive impairment that would interfere with your child being a good money manager, then your advisor may very well suggest you leave your assets to him or her in your will. However, if the opposite is the case, willing assets directly to your child may in some cases worsen his or her financial picture. In such a case, your estate expert may suggest establishing some kind of trust. There are dozens of types of trusts, and it's important to choose the one that best fits your situation.

For many parents who have a child with disabilities, a *special needs trust*, naming their child as a beneficiary with the trust administered by a third party is often the way to go. This type of trust keeps assets in a form that makes money available to your son or daughter without disqualifying him or her from government benefits that she or he would otherwise be eligible for. It is set up to provide supplemental funds that improve a disabled person's quality of life and are not designed to duplicate or replace governmental benefit programs. Since it follows strict requirements established by the government, including a prohibition against giving the beneficiary any kind of regular income, even a minor one, an experienced attorney should be consulted when drafting the trust documents.

An *inter vivos special needs trust* is typically a checking account set up while the parents are still alive that's used to pay a disabled person's supplementary expenses. A living special needs trust offers many benefits, including the ability to document expenses. This also allows relatives to gift amounts, thereby reducing their own estate taxes when the parents become incapacitated or die. Such a trust also allows for a smooth transition when the designated successor trustee takes over.

Depending on the type, your trust can be funded through a variety of means, including a direct transfer of money to the trustee by writing a check (payable to an individual identified as the trustee/payee in trust for the particular trust established), via a deed prepared by your attorney, or by a provision in your will. You could also use life insurance to fund a trust, or name the trustee of a trust as the recipient of an annuity, retirement plan, or other account payable upon your death. Be sure to consult an attorney or insurance professional to figure out the best way to transfer the funds into your trust.

"My brother is disabled. He's now in his fifties and is living with my mom, who is ninety. She's still going strong, but recently I've noticed my brother's bouts of depression and fits of anger are growing worse. I realize it's because he understands that mom won't be around forever, and who will take care of him? Where will he live? I've had to drop everything at the last minute and run over there to assure him that things will be OK. It's been causing a lot of disruption in the everyday life of my immediate family. So in the last year, I've started to work on a plan to transition my brother to a house of his own. I plan to purchase a duplex. My brother will live on the first floor, and my son, who is in college, will live on the second floor. That way my brother will have another family member close by as he transitions into his new home. When my son moves out after a few years, the income from the other unit will help pay the expenses. At some point, my brother will probably need additional in-home care, and I've scheduled a meeting with my other siblings to talk about how we can contribute funds to help pay for his future care, even after we're gone."   — *Maria, age 55*

PET-CARE PLANNING

According to the 2007-2008 National Pet Owners Survey, reported by the American Pet Products Manufacturers Association, 63 percent of U.S. households now own a pet. It's natural for those of us who enjoy the companionship and unconditional love of a loyal pet to fear what could happen if we are not around to take care of our four-legged friends. We worry that if something happens to us, and we don't have a plan in place to provide for the well-being of our pets, they could easily end up being euthanized. Many people who would love to have a pet forgo the pleasure as they get up in years, fearing what may happen to their pet if they become ill or die. It's too bad — studies reveal that having a pet contributes to mental health and well-being, helping to stave off the loneliness and depression that older adults can sometimes experience.

Fortunately, with a little careful planning, you can be assured that your beloved companion will be well taken care of if something does happen to you. At the time of publication, most of the states in the country have statutes on the books that allow people to establish trusts for their pets. Moreover, some pet advocacy organizations now offer retirement planning information that provides for pet care. In some cases, they even provide homes for pets whose owners can no longer take care of them. Concerned individuals are even getting into the act, offering kennels or "pet homes" specifically designed to take care of "retired" pets.

Pet Information Sheet

No matter what avenue you choose to take when planning for your pet's future care, the quality of that care will depend on the information you provide to the pet's designated caregiver. Create a "Pet Information Sheet" to pass this information along to the person who will ultimately be responsible for looking after your pet(s). Include a picture and the information below for each pet you have.

- ✓ Name and description (for example, breed, sex, birth date, color, markings, other distinguishing features)

- ✓ Where you obtained your pet (for example, the name of the shelter/ Humane Society, or a breeder's name and contact information)

✓ Veterinarian and other care providers' contact information (for example, trainer, groomer, farrier, pet sitter, dogwalker, daycare)

✓ Medical records, including spay and neuter information, vaccinations, allergies, medications

✓ Licensing and registrations (including whether an electronic chip was inserted)

✓ Location, if the pet doesn't reside with you (for example, the place where you board your horse)

✓ Feeding guidelines (frequency, time, type, and amount of food)

✓ Supplements or medications

✓ Routine care

✓ Other information (for example, potty spot, location of litter box, location of leash, travel kit, favorite toys, type of food bowl, etc.)

✓ Insurance information

Pet Trusts

A pet trust is a legal instrument designed to provide for the needs of your pets if you become unable to take care of them or after you are gone. You would set up the trust while you are still living. You, the trust "creator" (sometimes called the "grantor," "settlor," or "trustor," depending on the state) fund the trust with the amount of cash or other assets, such as property, that you've specified will be needed to care for your pet throughout his or her lifetime. The trust instrument itself may name an individual to enforce the trust, or, if no person is appointed, the court may appoint someone to enforce the trust (the "trustee") when the time comes. (The law may also allow for a person who has an interest in the animal's welfare to request the court to appoint a person to enforce the trust or to remove a person appointed.) When you are not capable of taking care of your pet, the trustee pays for your pet's care on an ongoing basis. The trust can be designed to provide for the care of a single animal, or for multiple animals. The trust terminates upon the death of the last surviving animal that the trust was established for.

Legal experts point out that an animal cannot be the beneficiary of a traditional trust and any arrangements ("pet trusts") that are made to care for a pet after someone dies are tenuous at best. Nevertheless, at the time of publication, thirty-nine states now have statutes providing for pet trusts; however, these statutes, and the degree to which they can be enforced, vary according to the state. In some cases, states designate pet trusts as "honorary" trusts, which allow the pet caretaker the option of giving the funds to the beneficiary (or beneficiaries) of your estate instead of honoring the terms of the trust. The hope is that the beneficiary then dispenses the funds on behalf of the pet. This option may be the only approach to take in a state where there is no legal means of establishing a pet trust and no way to enforce a pet trust. Be sure to check with your state's attorney general or with an animal welfare society in your state to determine what the law is where you live.

Budgeting for and Funding a Pet Trust

Fund the trust with the amount of money or just enough assets to cover your pet's needs, taking into account inflation. If you fund the trust with more assets than necessary to care for your pet(s), a court may declare the trust "excessive" and invalidate it. In such a case, if you are still living, the money might be returned to you, or, if you aren't alive, it might be given to those inheriting your estate. You may also wish to specify a budget or allocations for care in your will or trust document.

Alternatives to Pet Trusts

Conditional bequests give money to a specific person on condition that they utilize the funds to take care of your pet.

You can also bequeath your pet, plus the money to take care of it, to a specific person. You may also include trust provisions in your will (also known as a *testamentary trust*), but these provisions won't take place until you die and your will has been probated. This last option won't provide for your pet if you become disabled and doesn't cover the period of time between the time you die and the time your will is declared valid by a court when care of your pet will depend on the good will of a family member or friend.

Another possibility is to establish a *power of attorney* authorizing someone to take care of your pets if you become disabled or incapacitated.

Some animal sanctuaries, pet advocacy groups, and veterinary institutions offer for-a-fee-pet care programs, retirement homes, or placement services. You can sign your pet up for one of these retirement homes or plans and fund it prior to your death or donate your estate to an animal sanctuary on the condition that your pet will live there and be cared for until it in turn passes away. See Resources at the end of this chapter for some organizations that may be able to help you research this alternative. If you are interested in pursuing one of these options, however, be sure to visit the organization or pet care home to determine the quality and quantity of the staff, the living arrangements offered, physical plant, organizational standards and practices, and funding reserves before drafting a detailed agreement in writing. Have your attorney review the agreement before you sign it and incorporate it into your will.

How long will the trust remain in effect? A common law principle, the "rule against perpetuities" forbids trusts to last "forever," that is, for a significant time — usually twenty-one years — after the person who created the trust dies. Since some animals can be long-lived — cockatoos and other birds have been known to live as long as humans—this could present a problem with a pet. Section 408 of The Uniform Trust Code, a code approved and recommended by the National Conference of Commissioners on Uniform State Laws, makes an exception where pet trusts are concerned, allowing the trusts to continue for the life of the animal. While many states base their own Uniform Trust Acts on the Uniform Trust Code (UTC), individual states may substantially rewrite or decide not to adopt UTC provisions. If your pet is likely to live more than twenty-one years after you've established the trust, you should make a point of researching your state's law and speaking to an estate attorney about this concern.

Regarding tax liabilities, the IRS does not tax pet trusts in the same manner as it does other trusts. They are usually taxed at a lower rate than other trusts, and the schedule of applying tax to distributions is somewhat different. Talk to a tax attorney so you can understand how taxes will affect your trust.

Legal Look: Pet Ownership vs. Pet Guardianship

Pets are generally considered personal property under the law. By law, property owners enjoy certain rights and powers. Owners can sell, convey, or transfer property. But recently, pet advocacy groups have worked to change the term pet "owner" to "guardian" in local ordinances and state laws. As of the time of printing, twelve municipalities and the state of Rhode Island have enacted "pet guardian" laws. Biomedical research and veterinary science organizations have publicly opposed this trend. They point out that the term "guardian" has a specific legal definition and associated fiduciary responsibility and that using this specific term has far-reaching implications in how pets may be treated. Unlike property owners, guardians do not own the property. Guardians only temporarily possess property (their "ward'), and they must act as a trustee on behalf of it. If an animal becomes a "ward" of a "guardian" instead of an "owner's" piece of "property," then its rights under the law would change. Opponents to redefining pets as "wards" state that because decisions for wards must be made in the best interest of the ward, while decisions for property do not have to be, guardianship will put certain common procedures (such as transferring an animal to another party, euthanasia, spaying, neutering, and allowing an owner to have control over veterinary medical records) in jeopardy because such procedures "may not be considered to be in the best interest" of the animal. (*http://www. nabr.org/AnimalLaw/Guardianship/index.htm*) But one of the biggest reasons for opposing such changes in terminology appears to be its potential to reduce or eliminate research on animals. Opponents say the use of the term "guardian" will spur claims for the wrongful death of companion animals and the result could mirror the current sad state of affairs in human medicine; veterinarians would be forced to pay ever-higher malpractice insurance premiums, costs would rise, and fewer veterinarians would enter practice. While the debate continues to rage, some voices are calling for moderation. Charlotte Lacroix, D.V.M., J.D., a specialist in veterinary law and practice management, observes that "most people believe their pets are their best friend, as opposed to their children or their spouses. And that has very important legal consequences. If your pet is your best friend . . . you don't have a guardianship obligation."

LEGAL TERMS THAT RELATE TO DEPENDENT CARE

Charitable trusts: Trusts that benefit a charity, an entity, such as a monument, in general, or a social purpose, Unlike most trusts, a charitable trust may exist in perpetuity.

Charitable remainder unitrust: This kind of trust requires the trustee to be independent of the creator or beneficiary. A charitable remainder unitrust pays out to the named beneficiaries a fixed percentage of the trust's assets for a specified time period, after which the remainder goes to charity.

Clifford trust: A trust that provides income payable to a beneficiary for at least ten years. Upon termination, the principal reverts to the creator.

Conservatorship: *See Guardian.*

Corpus: *See Principal.*

Custodial gift: A gift to a minor child from an adult that is managed by the giver, or another adult appointed to the giver, until the child is legally of age to become responsible for the gift.

Declaration of trust: The document signed by a person to create a trust. In addition to an assertion that assets are being held for the benefit of one or more people or another entity, it typically outlines the terms of the trust, including who the beneficiaries of the trust are, how the assets placed into it will be managed, how profits, if any, will be distributed, and the name of the person appointed to manage the trust (i.e., the *trustee*).

Discretionary trust: Allows the trustee authority to exercise his or her discretion in making distributions to the beneficiary.

Fiduciary: The individual, company, or other entity that holds and manages assets on behalf of the trust's income beneficiary.

Guardian: A legal means of granting a designated adult the power to make decisions for someone (a "ward") who is considered unable to make decisions himself or herself, such as a minor child (that is, a child who has not yet turned eighteen or been legally married). There are different types of guardians. For example, a "guardian of the estate" or "conservator" usually has complete discretion to make living arrangements, manage finances, and make medical decisions for someone deemed incapable. A limited conservator or guardian is often appointed for those with developmental disabilities or other special needs. In this case, the guardian only has powers over those areas that the disabled individual cannot manage on his or her own.

Honorary trust: An arrangement whereby assets of a trust are assigned to an individual to be used for a specified non-charitable purpose, but because no beneficiary exists who can enforce the trust, whether the trust will be implemented according to its creator's wishes is simply up to the trustee. Simply put, this kind of trust depends on the "honor" of the trustee to enforce the wishes of the person who set up the trust.

Income beneficiary: One who is designated to receive income from a trust during the term of the trust.

Inter vivos trust: *See Living trust.*

Irrevocable trust: A trust that can never be changed except with the consent of all beneficiaries.

Life estate: An estate or interest in real property, which is held for the duration of the life of some certain person or entity.

Living trust: A trust established between two or more individuals that takes place while the trustor is still living. Also called an *inter vivos trust.* In many living trusts the creator of the trust names her- or himself as the original trustee so he or she won't lose control of the assets. Then, in the declaration of trust document, you name the person or organization who will inherit the trust property after you die (the *successor trustee*). This way the assets of the trust pass outside a will and no probate court processions are required.

Pour-over will: A will that leaves some or all of the will-maker's estate assets to a trust established while he or she is still alive.

Principal: The property in a trust.

Revocable trust: The creator retains the power to revoke (annul, abolish, rescind) the trust.

Spendthrift trust: A trust that is created for the benefit of someone who is a poor money manager. The beneficiary is paid income from the trust, but the trust's assets cannot be tapped to pay the spendthrift's debts (although the beneficiary can use the income to pay bills). So, for example, if a beneficiary gets a $3,000 a month income from the trust and the beneficiary makes a purchase of $25,000 on a credit card, he or she cannot withdraw $25,000 from the trust to pay the credit card bill, but would be able to pay $3,000 a month out of the monthly income towards the bill.

SSI representative payee: Under certain circumstances, the Federal Supplemental Social Security Income Program (SSI) allows for a representative to receive and disburse SSI funds to eligible SSI beneficiaries.

Testamentary trust: A trust that is created by including specific language in a will and that takes effect upon the death of the person who established it. For example, someone might include language in a will to the effect that "the residue of my estate shall form the *corpus* (body) of a trust" and from there go on to name the trustee, beneficiary, and other terms of the trust.

Trust: A legal entity created to hold assets for the benefit of certain persons or entities, typically documented in a written declaration of trust that names the trustees and describes the trust's terms and conditions.

Trust beneficiary: A person or entity who is named to enjoy a beneficial interest in the trust.

Trustee: The person or entity that holds the assets, managing them and the trust according to the terms outlined in the declaration of trust, and who also distributes the assets to the beneficiaries.

RESOURCES

Help for Caregivers

The Arc®
Help for people with intellectual and developmental disabilities
Web site: www.thearc.org

The Alzheimer's Disease Education and Referral (ADEAR)
Web site: www.alzheimers.org

American Parkinson's Disease Association (APDA)
Web site: www.apdaparkinson.org

Autism Society of America™
Web site: www.autism-society.org

Beverly Foundation
566 El Dorado St., #100, Pasadena, CA 91101
Phone: 626-792-2292; Fax: 626-792-6117
Web site: www.beverlyfoundation.org

Children of Aging Parents (CAPS)
P.O. Box 167, Richboro, PA 18954
Phone: 800-227-7294
Web site: www.caps4caregivers.org

DisabilityInfo.gov
Phone: 800-333-4636
Web site: www.disabilityinfo.gov

Disabled and Alone/Life Services for the Handicapped, Inc.
61 Broadway, Suite 510, New York, NY 10006
Phone: (800) 995-0066; Fax: (212) 532-3588
Web site: www.disabledandalone.org

Eldercare Locater
Phone: 800-677-1116
Web site: www.eldercare.gov

Estate and Life Planning for Disabled Dependents Association for Persons with Severe Handicaps (TASH)
29 W. Susquehanna Avenue, Suite 210, Baltimore, MD 21204
Phone: 410-828-8274

Family Caregiver Alliance®, National Center on Caregiving
180 Montgomery St., Suite 1100, San Francisco, CA 94104
Phone: 415-434-3388; 800-445-8106; Fax: 415-434-3508
Web site: www.caregiver.org

Judge David L. Bazelon Center for Mental Health Law
1101 15th Street NW, Ste.1212, Washington, D.C. 20005-5002
Phone: 202-467-5730; Fax: 202-223-0409
Web site: www.bazelon.org

National Adult Day Services
85 South Washington, Suite 316, Seattle, Washington, 20008
Phone: 800-558-5301; Fax: 202-783-2255
Web site: www.nadsa.org

National Alliance on Mental Illness (NAMI)
Web site: www.nami.org

National Association of State Units on Aging (NASUA)
1201 15th St, NW, Suite 350, Washington, D.C. 20005
Phone: 202-898-2578; Fax: 202-898-2583
Web site: www.nasua.org

National Dissemination Center for Children with Disabilities (NICHCY)
P.O. Box 1492, Washington, DC 20013
Phone: 800-695-0285, 202-884-8200; Fax: 202-884-8441
Web site: www.nichcy.org

National Down Syndrome Congress
Web site: www.ndsccenter.org

National Down Syndrome Society
Web site: www.ndss.org

National Easter Seal Society
Web site: www.easterseals.com

National Family Caregivers Association (NFCA)
10400 Connecticut Avenue, #500, Kensington, MD 20895-3944
Phone: 800-896-3650; 301-942-6430; Fax: 301-942-2302
Web site: www.nfcacares.org

SPRY Foundation
13916 Rosemary Street, Chevy Chase, MD 20815
Phone: 301-656-3405; Fax: 301-656-6221
Web site: www.spry.org

Today's Caregiver™
3005 Greene Street, Hollywood, FL 33020
Phone: 954-893-0550, 800-829-2734; Fax: 954-893-1779
Web site: caregiver.com

United Cerebral Palsy™
Web site: www.ucp.org

PETS

The Estate Planning for Pets Foundation
3159 E. Beardsley, Box 1091, Phoenix, Arizona 85050
Web site: www.estateplanningforpets.org

International Association of Pet Cemeteries
and Crematoria
P.O. Box 163, 5055 Route 11, Ellenburg Depot, NY 12935
Phone: 518-594-3000; Fax: 518-594-8801
Web site: www.iaopc.com

NB Pet Trusts
Phone: 1-800-889-9005
Web site: http://www.nbpettrusts.com/index.asp?p=sign_up

Pet Guardian LLC Pet Trust Plans
Web site: www.petguardian.com

Chapter 6:
A Final Celebration

My Documents at-a-Glance

Fill in the chart below to keep track of where your critical documents will be stored and who will have access to them.

DOCUMENT	LOCATION	ACCESS/COPY GIVEN TO
Burial lot deed		
Funeral instructions		
Funeral provider documentation (general price list, receipts)		
Funeral payment documents including contracts, receipts, or special instructions (e.g., trusts)		

Psychologists who rate stressful life events tell us that the death of a loved one, especially a spouse, is at the top of the list. However, people who know that their loved one is dying (due to a long-term illness) are able to cope better than those who experience a loved one dying unexpectedly. So talking about death, while it is not something our culture embraces, can help you to deal with it.

Talking about death also allows us to take care of unfinished business so that we ourselves can feel some sense of completion. What are you not doing that you want to do? What are you not saying that you want to say? Acknowledging that our current lives will end someday, opens us up to answering these important questions. How we approach our final time on this planet — what we think, what we say, how we act, and how we interact with others — is our choice. Whether we will live fifty years longer or only fifty minutes longer, we can choose to make the most of our remaining time.

Instead of running from death's limitation, we can embrace it as an opportunity to use our gifts well and to give back to others. As a friend who lost her dearly loved husband once put it to me, "A person's character is revealed most in how he or she faces the indignity of illness and the finality of death. That really tells you everything about them as a person." Every minute counts, and every action counts. Putting your affairs in order, including making funeral arrangements, is one way to demonstrate your care and concern, and to celebrate your love for those you leave behind.

KEEPING YOUR DOCUMENTS SAFE

This chart will help you determine where to store your important funeral documents.

DOCUMENT	LOCATION
Burial lot deed	Safe deposit box
Funeral instructions	Signed original with lawyer or in a fireproof storage container at home
Statement of funeral goods and services selected	Signed original with lawyer or in a fireproof storage container at home
Funeral general price list	With lawyer or in a fireproof storage container at home
Receipts, payments, funeral savings or trust papers (to pay for funeral)	Trust documents are typically kept with lawyer. Documents needed immediately should be kept with lawyer or in fireproof container at home. Provide copies to your estate's trustee.

—From the Expert—————————————————

Reverend Glenn H. Asquith, Jr., Ph.D., on addressing issues from a spiritual perspective

As chair of the Pastoral Theology Department at Moravian Theological Seminary, Bethlehem, Pennsylvania, Reverend Glenn H. Asquith, Jr., has had in-depth training in behavioral health, psychology, and theology. As a pastoral counselor, he combines this knowledge to help people understand and address issues that arise in life from a spiritual perspective. He often finds himself in nursing homes and hospitals, counseling people with serious illnesses and with end-of-life concerns. Below he offers some of his insights.

- **Advance directives can make end-of-life care easier because it's a way of letting your loved ones know that by stopping heroic measures, they are doing what mom or dad would have wanted.** However, when you create an advance directive, you'll need to choose a person who can advocate for you, but that person should not necessarily be a spouse or a child. Often, children are not ready to let a parent die, and they fight with the health care providers and even against the advance directive. If the children have unfinished business with a parent, that can come into play, too.

- I've witnessed a lot of good experiences with hospice care. It's a wonderful way to go, surrounded by family and pets and in familiar surroundings. **Hospice care provides a combination of services to people — nursing, social work, and even chaplaincy. It allows a person to die normally at home. Its use is growing, not just at home but also in the hospital setting,** although that's still an exception. In the institutional setting, it takes the form of minimal care with some pain management.

- People may opt for hospice and then decide to go for additional treatments, in which case they take themselves out of hospice. My father didn't leave the nursing home for the last three weeks of his life, and just received minimal fluids and morphine. But at one point before that, he wanted to get another transfusion, and he had to understand that he wouldn't be able to be "in hospice" any more if he was being actively treated.

- **One of the questions I often ask of people who are preparing to die is, "Do you have anything that you really need to say to your son, your daughter? Now is the time."** I make sure to ask how I can help to arrange those conversations. To take care of any unfinished business, to say the things that need to be said, makes the healing easier afterwards for those we leave behind.

- **It's very common for people to do a life review right at the end.** It's done several ways. Some people do it by telling stories about where they lived and what they did, and what they overcame. It's a way of acknowledging to themselves that they did accomplish things in their lifetime. Erik Erikson talked about old age overcoming despair, about ending our lives with a sense of integrity. Caregivers, social workers, and pastors who comfort those at end-of-life would do well to help foster the life review by encouraging reminiscing. Photo albums, a scrapbook, memoir, or tape of personal reminiscences are ways of doing "the review," and will be treasured by survivors.

PLANNING A FUNERAL

People often include funeral instructions in their wills, but there are no guarantees those instructions will be followed because the will is usually read and probated after the funeral itself occurs. To ensure that arrangements are in place that will follow your wishes and will reduce stress on those left behind, many industry experts advise preplanning your own funeral.

Plan to shop around and visit several providers. Costs tend to vary greatly, and it's also helpful to choose a place that can offer personal services in a sympathetic and understanding way. After you've made your arrangements, keep your paperwork in a safe place *(see Chapter 1 for suggestions)* and give copies of it to a family member, friend, or other individual. Also, consider holding a family conference to communicate your wishes and plans to your loved ones.

Options for Your Final Celebration

Before you go shopping, spend some time thinking about the kind of funeral you want. Choices include an *immediate burial* without a formal ceremony, viewing, or visit with the body, though this could include a grave side service. *Direct cremation* usually doesn't include any formal ceremony. A *funeral ceremony* is a service honoring the deceased's memory with the body present. A *memorial service* is a service honoring the deceased's memory without the body present.

Of course, if you belong to a particular religion, that can influence your decision about how your final passage should be celebrated. Some traditions call for a nighttime wake or viewing of the body followed the next day by a formal service at a church or the funeral home, after which the body is transported to a cemetery for internment. Other traditions call for immediate burial with a ceremony, which is then followed by family members undergoing a ritualized mourning period. Another tradition may call for a lengthy wake over several days, followed by cremation. You can include your preferences for your burial and funeral in a letter of intent to your loved ones.

In addition to informing any rituals or ceremonies that will be followed, the customs of faith will influence many of the details of funeral planning. Many people still opt for a traditional burial, especially those whose religions preclude cremation. However, because cremation does a better job at preserving land, many consider it to be a greener alternative than burial. Cremation can also be a less expensive option, especially if it involves a small or biodegradable container.

If you opt for burial, you'll need to choose a cemetery, plot, and marker or gravestone. Cemeteries often have restrictions on the size, shape, and type of grave marker, as well as the kinds of materials they'll accept. You may wish to follow in the steps of literary figures, such as Nobel Prize-winning poet William Butler Yeats, who famously chose his own headstone inscription, but keep in mind that cemeteries with religious affiliations may also restrict what mottos can be put on the gravestone, limiting them to verses from the Bible or other religious text.

If you decide on cremation, you'll need to make certain other choices — deciding between a funeral home that provides cremation services or a cremation society, whether your final resting place will be an urn or special container, a regular burial plot or smaller cremation plot, or if you'd prefer to have your ashes scattered in a specific area. Due to the increasing popularity of cremation, some municipalities have now designated areas for this very purpose. Be sure to ask the authorities if the scattering of ashes is allowed (some prohibit this) and whether a permit is required. Another option is to request that your ashes be scattered at a place that has meaning for you, such as out at sea if you enjoyed sailing. Some funeral providers offer special plane flights and the like for distributing cremated remains.

Personalizing Your Funeral

It comes as a surprise to many that there are alternatives to holding a traditional funeral or even to holding the service at a traditional funeral home. Most states allow home funerals, and some even allow the family to manage the funeral as long as all applicable laws are followed. Burial at sea is a dream of many boatmen, military and civilian, and these days, there is even a company that will incorporate remains into a reef to support ocean life. Donating your body to science is another option that may have meaning for you. But even if you decide to hold the funeral at a traditional funeral home, you may wish to make a few changes that will make your funeral as meaningful as possible for those left behind or, if you are a survivor planning it, a more personalized celebration of your loved one's uniqueness. These might include playing favorite music, even if it is lively, holding a memorial service at a favorite location, placing favorite items in the casket, Webcasting the funeral, planting a memorial tree or garden, or creating a personalized Web page in celebration of the life lived. If you find it difficult to say goodbye to everyone in person, consider making a memory book, photo collage, or album. Another option is to make a video of yourself sharing your thoughts and saying goodbye to your children, grandchildren and other loved ones, so they will have a personal keepsake to turn to in the years ahead. Survivors also may wish to create a memorial video to play at the wake and to keep as a memento. Most funeral homes today offer this service.

Charitable Donations at a Funeral

Charitable donations are another way to personalize your final celebration and leave a legacy at the same time. If you have a favorite charity, you could request donations to that organization in lieu of flowers or ask that a donation request be placed in your funeral notice or obituary. Giving to charity at the time of death is often encouraged in some religions, and funeral homes usually can assist with donation cards and donation services.

The Military Funeral

Regardless of rank or their burial location, all honorably discharged or current veterans qualify for military honors at their funerals. This typically involves a flag, provided free of charge to drape the casket or accompany the veteran's urn, two uniformed military personnel to fold and present the flag (it's usually given to the next-of-kin as a keepsake), and the playing of Taps either by a live bugler or via a CD. If you are working with a funeral director, he or she can arrange for military honors by calling 1-877-MIL-HONR (645-4667). The Department of Veterans Affairs (VA) provides a sum of money to help cover expenses (this can range from a few hundred to more than a thousand dollars, depending on whether it's a service-related death or not). The VA also provides a grave marker for eligible veterans who are being buried in a military or other qualified cemetery. Veterans may be buried in national cemeteries where space is available. Inurnment (having your ashes placed in an urn or other container) is free for veterans at the Columbarium at Arlington National Cemetery in Virginia. A relative or friend of the deceased veteran may apply through their local VA office for a *presidential memorial certificate (PMC)*, a certificate signed by the president that expresses the country's grateful recognition of the veteran's service. Eligible recipients (typically a relative or friend) may apply through the nearest VA regional office. Call 1-800-827-1000 or visit www.military.com for more information about VA death benefits and programs, including eligibility requirements.

A Legal Look at the Funeral Rule

Reports of profiteering by unscrupulous funeral providers preying on the bereaved sparked activists to lobby for federal regulation of the industry. In 1984 the Federal Trade Commission (FTC) passed the Funeral Rule, a set of guidelines designed to ensure that funeral providers offer accurate price quotes and certain disclosures about funeral goods and services. Under this rule, funeral providers may not engage in deceptive or unfair practices, including:

- misrepresenting legal, crematory, and cemetery requirements

- embalming for a fee without permission

- requiring the purchase of a casket for direct cremation

- requiring consumers to buy certain funeral goods or services as a condition for furnishing other funeral goods or services.

The Funeral Rule was also designed to ensure that consumers could effectively comparison shop funeral goods and services and purchase only those items that they want.

WORKING WITH A FUNERAL PROVIDER

Whichever method you choose — burial or cremation — you'll want to decide whether to leave most of the arrangements to the funeral provider (after expressing your own preferences) or to go further and actually plan the details of your own funeral yourself. This can be difficult for some people, but others prefer to undertake the planning so that their loved ones won't have to think about such matters in what presumably will be a time of grief for them. By taking care of all of these details yourself in advance, you can give your loved ones time to draw together as a family, and prevent some of those arguments that can occur when such arrangements must be made at a time of great stress.

If you opt for a funeral, naturally you'll want to choose a funeral provider who is easy to work with and reputable. Start by asking people for recommendations. Beyond that, look for a certified funeral provider. For information about trade groups that certify funeral providers and adhere to certain codes of ethics, see the Resources section at the end of this chapter.

A good funeral director is more than a sales person; he or she also is somewhat of a psychologist, able to exude a comforting presence for those dealing with this difficult subject. But keep in mind that funeral planning must take into account practical matters also, such as cost.

Fortunately, the law provides for many of these practical matters, so that most of us don't have to remind ourselves to ask about them when we are dealing with the highly emotional nature of making funeral arrangements. One of the most important items required by law is the free *general price list (GPL)*. Funeral providers must give this price list to any consumer who inquires about such services in a face-to-face meeting, whether in the funeral home, at home, or in a nursing home.

The funeral provider must provide you with a take-away list, itemizing goods and services. In the event that you preplan your funeral and your survivors decide to add a service, or in cases where a prepaid plan didn't come with a guarantee of fees at the time of death, the funeral provider must also provide the survivors with the relevant price list and a Statement of Funeral Goods and Services Selected. While federal law requires the list be produced in a face-to-face meeting, some states also require providers to mail similar lists in response to phone or mail inquiries.

In addition to pricing, the law requires certain important disclosure information to protect the consumer's right to shop around as well as to purchase only those items desired by the consumer or required by law (although the provider can provide packages in addition to itemized services). Consumer rights and protections detailed by the rule include the right to choose an alternative container (as opposed to a presumably more expensive casket) for cremation, to refuse embalming except where required by law, and to purchase a casket from a seller of one's choice.

However, not every provider is required to offer all items or services, and funeral providers may charge a "non-declinable" fee to cover their basic services and overhead. These fees may be included in some items on the list, and, where they are, an explanation must be provided. Before purchasing any item, be sure you understand any applicable warranties. The funeral provider should also inform you of any manufacturer's warranties.

But keep in mind that, although the FTC has set requirements for funeral providers, it does not mandate or set pricing. Prices for services and goods can vary significantly depending on the provider. Some reports have found that while a basic funeral may cost as little as a couple of thousand dollars, it's not unusual for a traditional funeral to cost closer to $15,000. Think carefully about your needs and shop around to get the best value for your money.

At the end of the meeting to discuss arrangements, the funeral provider must give you a Statement of Funeral Goods and Services Selected. If arrangements are made over the phone, the provider must send you a statement as soon as possible. The statement must itemize each of the goods and services. A funeral director may arrange and pay for certain third-party services on your behalf, such as death certificates, public transportation, flowers, gratuities, music, death notices to be published in the paper, death certificates, and more. The statement should identify and provide a "good faith" estimate for any such items on the statement that must be paid for by "cash advance." Be sure to get and review a list of itemized charges for the total cost of the services and goods, including "cash advance" items and commissions or service fees for procuring them, before you pay the final bill. Keep these important documents together with your letter of intent (describing how you want your burial and remains to be handled) in a safe place, such as with your will at your attorney's office.

PAYING FOR A FUNERAL

Whether or not you decide to plan your own funeral, you may decide to save your loved ones some money and expense by creating a funeral payment plan.

Many people simply choose to leave it to their heirs to pay for their funeral out of the estate, but this approach may end up reducing the estate because such funds are subject to inheritance tax. In addition, if the deceased's accounts or estate is frozen at the time of death, the beneficiaries may have to pay for the funeral out of their own pockets and wait until the estate is probated until they can be reimbursed, which may be somewhat inconvenient for your loved ones.

Once you have some idea of the arrangements and their cost, you can assess the options for paying for them. If you are or were in the military, the military will provide for some benefits (*see "The Military Funeral" on p.123*), so these will need to be factored into any amounts set aside for the funeral and burial costs. Also, Social Security benefits provide for a one-time lump sum death benefit (a little over $200 at this printing) to the surviving spouse, and your spouse and children, if you have them, may qualify for other benefits. Note that various organizations may offer benefits or reduced fees for the deceased. Civic organizations and church groups sometimes offer burial benefits, and local governments sometimes reduce the cost of inurnment for residents who are cremated or they will allow ashes to be scattered for free in specific areas.

In addition, you may want to consider doing one or more of the following:

Buy some items in advance. Many people buy their cemetery plots in advance of their death. You can also buy items such as a casket in advance, and have a funeral provider store it for you if necessary.

Take out an insurance policy. Funeral insurance policies specifically designed to cover funeral-related costs are available, though they often cover only items that are itemized in the policy. Some funeral providers even offer such insurance. Typically, funeral insurance is offered with a term, similar to many term life insurance products. Another option is to buy a life insurance policy that will specifically be used to cover your funeral expenses (instructions should be left to your beneficiary to follow this request). Your employer may also automatically provide employer-sponsored life insurance that could be applied to a funeral; if the basic benefit amount is not enough to cover expenses, you may be able to pay an additional modest sum to increase the benefit. Some life insurance policies also contain an *accelerated death benefits (ADB)* clause allowing you to collect or borrow all or a part of the policy's death benefit in advance, which is useful if you are nearing death. Insurance offers many benefits, allowing you to fund your funeral; some policies accrue interest, which provides a hedge against inflation; and there may be tax advantages as well. However, shop carefully: not all policies offer the same benefits for the same price, and some may reduce or change benefits as you increase in age.

Set up a *payable on death (POD)/transferable on death (TOD) account/Totten trust:* You can transfer money or property, such as stocks and bonds, without going through probate by setting up certain kinds of accounts with named beneficiaries. Taxes are generally incurred on these accounts, but a benefit is that, unlike a pre-need or prepayment funeral account, they can be canceled or amended without any penalties. Be sure to ask the bank or other provider whether the account is insured against bank failure through the Federal Deposit Insurance Corporation (FDIC).

Pre-need trusts: Trust accounts may be fully funded or set up to be funded with monthly payments. Ask who manages the trust and what their track record is; ideally, your investment should increase over time (although you'll also pay taxes on the income). Be sure to ask what happens if you die prematurely: Will your family have to make up any difference in the trust? Will your funeral expenses be covered? What happens if the trust grows so that there is money left over once your funeral is paid for?

Pay in advance: You can sign a contract with your funeral provider and pay all, or part, of your funeral costs in advance. Before doing so, check the laws of your state, which govern such transactions. In some states, the funeral provider is required to buy a life insurance policy with the money, listing the funeral provider as the policy's beneficiary. Other states require a percentage of the money to be deposited in a trust regulated by the state. But many states offer little protection to the consumer, so be careful before choosing this option. Treat it as you would any financial transaction, and choose a provider that has been recommended to you by someone you trust; make sure the agreement is spelled out in writing and that you understand it; have them provide a receipt for the money you've provided and written confirmation of where it has been deposited. Interest earned on the money should be reported to you every January (you will need to pay taxes on it). Be aware that some charges may be "non-guaranteed," which means that fees for the items and services you've chosen are charged at the rates existing at the time of your funeral. If the amount you've paid and the interest on it do not cover expenses at the time of death, your estate will be charged the difference.

A *viatical* is an agreement whereby someone, usually with a terminal disease, sells his or her life insurance policy at a discount from its face value for cash and a buyer (often an investment company) cashes in the full amount of the policy once the original owner dies. When you evaluate your insurance, you may come across phrases such as "viatical settlements," "life settlements," "living benefits," or "senior settlements," which explain these types of benefits. Most experts say this is an option to avoid — essentially, you're betting on your own death, and so is the company reimbursing you for the money. However, some groups, such as AIDS Project Los Angeles (APLA), provide guidance about them, pointing out that these policies may be an important source of cash for terminally ill people (see http://www.apla.org/programs/benefits/viatical.html). The California State Department of Insurance also provides information about viatical settlements, noting that life-threatening or catastrophic illnesses can present one of life's greatest challenges. Under such circumstances, all options for funding may need to be considered.

Don't Forget to Ask . . .

When deciding among the various payment options for a funeral, be sure to ask your funeral provider:

✓ What happens in the event that the funeral provider goes out of business or files bankruptcy?

✓ What protections are in place for ensuring the security of your funds?

✓ What protections are in place to guarantee the cost of the services? (For example, is there a price guarantee? Is the money invested to protect against inflation?)

✓ If you move, is the money or plan transferable?

✓ Is the funeral provider bound to use the entire amount set aside for the contracted-for services, and if not, what happens to the balance?

✓ Is there a "back-out" clause in case you change your mind about the arrangements you've paid for, and what, if any, penalties are associated with it?

✓ If your family accidentally pays for a funeral service either at the same facility you've contracted with or elsewhere, what happens to the services you purchased/your prepayments?

✓ What happens if services other than the ones planned for need to be purchased?

✓ Is there any time limit associated with the payment plan, or any age or time limit with the funeral insurance plan? For example, will you be covered only for ten years, or until your die, if you happen to live longer than expected? What, if any, penalties are there?

✓ Don't forget to let your attorney, estate executor, and family members know if you've prearranged to pay for your funeral; otherwise, they may use other funds to cover the arrangements.

LEAVING A LEGACY

When we leave a legacy, we no longer see death as such a final act. While we may no longer be around to engage directly in life, we can still influence those who are alive through our legacy. It can capture our best hopes and help to ensure we are in some way continuing to affect our loved ones and organizations and institutions we believe in for the better.

Our legacy may simply be the principles and guidances we've passed on to the children we've brought into the world. For those of us who do not have children, our legacy may be the good works that we did, a charity we supported or a trust we created to benefit the world in some way. Or it may be the artwork, garden, or the warm, inviting home we created and shared with others. Or it simply may be our spirit that we shared. It would be great if we lived every moment of our lives thinking about our legacy — our giving to the world — but often our legacy gets pushed aside in the effort it takes just to get through the business of an ordinary day. Understanding what we are here to do, and what we have done, seems to come to most of us only in quiet moments of reflection. As we contemplate our own mortality, we discover the richness of our lives — memories that are unexpected treasures at a time that could otherwise be filled with sorrow and uncertainty. If we haven't taken the time before, now is the time to decide what our legacy will be. We can think about how we wish to share our thoughts and experiences and dreams with those we love, perhaps in the form of a memoir or letters.

The form on the next page can serve as a guide to letting your heart speak its deepest feelings to your family and friends — whether you write this letter now or in the future. It will be a gift you leave behind for them.

Legacy Letter to Friends and Loved Ones

Putting your thoughts on paper to those you care about most.

Dear_____,

I remember how we met:_____

_____

_____

_____

_____

My fondest memories of you are:_____

_____

_____

_____

_____

Over the years I have come to appreciate these things about you: _____

_____

_____

_____

_____

Please forgive me for:_____

_____

_____

_____

_____

What I treasure the most about our relationship is:_____

_____

_____

_____

_____

What I wish for your future:_____

_____

_____

_____

_____

I've always wanted to share this with you:_____   _____

_____

_____

_____

_____

Thank you for:_____

_____

_____

_____

_____

You've meant a lot to me.

Love,

[Your Name]

LIVING WELL UNTIL THE END

Studies show that most people want to pass away peacefully in a familiar setting without pain, surrounded by the people they love. Unfortunately, other studies indicate that all too many of us end up dying suddenly in unfamiliar and stressful hospital settings because we haven't taken the time to plan for unforeseen circumstances. We can't know when we'll die, or who will be there, or whether our family doctor will even be the one treating us, or if it will be unknown emergency room doctors or an unfamiliar specialist. But with some planning, we can tip the odds in our favor. We can think about health care options ahead of time, when we are in a calm frame of mind and capable of making rational decisions. We can draft documents that will help protect our interests and communicate our wishes should we become unable to do so. And we can enlist the help of a personal health representative and authorize that individual to make treatment and care decisions on our behalf. We can request that we be surrounded by comfort and beauty as we say our final goodbyes.

My Vision for a Beautiful Ending

No matter how long you've lived or how much time you've spent with your loved ones, you may find it difficult to convey your deepest feelings and wishes to them. Here are some sentences to fill in that can help you communicate your feelings, concerns, and wishes to your loved ones and share your values, hopes, and dreams.

When I die, my ideal scenario would be to die at this location:_____

_____

I would like to be surrounded by these people and things:_____

_____

I would be happy knowing that:_____

_____

Before I die, I want to be sure:

I tell _____ that I love him/her/them.

I forgive others: _____

_____

I forgive myself for: _____

_____

I want to be remembered for: _____ _____

_____

I'd like to share these memories with my loved ones:_____

_____

_____ _____

I offer thanks for:_____ _____

_____

I want my friends and loved ones to enjoy: _____ _____

_____ _____

I'd like the following to happen (this can be as specific as "I'd like cousin Johnny to water his rose bush" or as universal as "I want there to be fewer wars in the world"):

____ _____

_____

The things I value most are:_____ _____

_____

Words of wisdom I have found valuable include:_____

_____

For those who I leave behind, I offer these final words and thoughts:_____

_____

_____

PLANNING AHEAD TO MAKE THE MOST OF YOUR TIME NOW

Congratulations to you for reaching the end of this book, for giving thought to how to organize your affairs for daily living and for dying. Death is inevitable, life is impermanent. Therefore, it makes sense for us to take advantage of every minute we are alive. By addressing those issues that can tie up our time and resources, we free ourselves to enjoy those precious minutes of life. We no longer have to spend energy putting things out of our mind that we'd rather not deal with, or living with an undertow of fear and concern for ourselves and our loved ones, and feeling disempowered. We can move forward from this point on, satisfied that we have done our best to provide for those we care about, enjoying what the time ahead has to offer. We may need to cycle back to these difficult choices and topics again to ensure that they reflect the realities of life at a given moment in time, but we can do so with the knowledge that we'll find those decisions much easier to deal with in the future — because we chose to spend time on them now.

RESOURCES

Funeral Consumers Alliance
33 Patchen Road, South Burlington, VT 05403
Phone: 800-765-0107
Web site: www.funerals.org

Complying With the Funeral Rule
Publication available online from the Federal Trace Commission at:
Web site: http://www.ftc.gov/bcp/conline/pubs/buspubs/funeral.pdf

Funerals: A Consumer Guide
Publication available online from the Federal Trade Commission at
Web site: http://www.ftc.gov/bcp/conline/pubs/services/funeral.shtm

International Cemetery, Cremation, and Funeral Association (ICCFA)
107 Carpenter Dr., Suite 100, Sterling, VA 20164
Phone: 800-645-7700, 703-391-8400; Fax: 703-391-8416

Funeral and Memorialization Information Council
13625 Bishop's Drive, Brookfield, WI 53005
Phone: 262-814-1545; Fax: 262-789-6977
Web site: www.famic.org

International Order of the Golden Rule (OGR®)
P.O. Box 28689, St. Louis, MO 63146-1189
Phone: 800-637-8030; Fax: 314-209-1289
Web site: www.ogr.org

Redwood Funeral Society
P. O. Box 7501, Cotati, CA 94931
Phone: 707-568-7684
Web site: www.funeral.org

VIATICALS

California Department of Insurance
(Supplies an online list of viatical providers. They also have a consumer hotline you can contact at 800-927-HELP)
Web site: www.insurance.ca.gov

New York State Insurance Department
(Also provides an online list of viatical providers. The consumer hotline number is 212-480-6400)
Web site: www.ins.state.ny.us

Index